KU-731-304

BRIDGE IS FUN

So you want to improve your bridge game . . . and you think you might need quite a while to achieve that? Then this is the book for you. Not only will you find challenging problems on all areas of the game, bidding with or without interference, opening leads, declarer play and defence, but you will also find the lighter side of bridge following most of the solutions to the problems.

How will that help you? Why include these irreverent comments? The aim is to make you smile, perhaps laugh, as you work through each of the problems. The bridge aspect is designed to stimulate you and hone your bridge skills. If you have a chuckle here and there at the not-so-serious material, then there is every chance that you will live longer and so have more time to improve your game even further.

Laughter is indeed the best medicine and a happy bridge player is also a better bridge player. Work at the bridge, enjoy the many incongruities and absurdities, let yourself go.

Ron Klinger is a leading international bridge teacher and has represented Australia in many world championships from 1976 to 2003. He has written over forty books, some of which have been translated into Bulgarian, Chinese, Danish, French, Hebrew and Icelandic.

by RON KLINGER *in the Master Bridge Series*

BETTER BRIDGE WITH A BETTER MEMORY
THE POWER OF SHAPE • WHEN TO BID, WHEN TO PASS
*GUIDE TO BETTER CARD PLAY • PLAYING TO WIN AT BRIDGE
*Winner of the 1991 *Book of the Year Award* of the American Bridge Teachers' Association
GUIDE TO BETTER ACOL BRIDGE • 5-CARD MAJORS • POWER ACOL
GUIDE TO BETTER DUPLICATE BRIDGE • CUE-BIDDING TO SLAMS
BRIDGE CONVENTIONS, DEFENCES & COUNTERMEASURES
100 WINNING BRIDGE TIPS • 50 MORE WINNING BRIDGE TIPS
100 WINNING DUPLICATE TIPS • ACOL BRIDGE MADE EASY
THE MODERN LOSING TRICK COUNT • ACOL BRIDGE FLIPPER
IMPROVE YOUR BRIDGE MEMORY • PRACTICAL SLAM BIDDING
THE LAW OF TOTAL TRICKS FLIPPER • BASIC ACOL BRIDGE FLIPPER
DUPLICATE BRIDGE FLIPPER • 5-CARD MAJORS FLIPPER
20 GREAT CONVENTIONS FLIPPER • BRIDGE IS FUN
MODERN LOSING TRICK COUNT FLIPPER
BID BETTER, MUCH BETTER AFTER OPENING 1NT

with Pat Husband and Andrew Kambites
BASIC BRIDGE: The Guide to Good Acol Bidding and Play

with David Bird
KOSHER BRIDGE • KOSHER BRIDGE 2
THE RABBI'S MAGIC TRICK: More Kosher Bridge

with Andrew Kambites
BRIDGE CONVENTIONS FOR YOU
CARD PLAY MADE EASY 1: Safety Plays and Endplays
CARD PLAY MADE EASY 2: Know Your Suit Combinations
CARD PLAY MADE EASY 3: Trump Management
CARD PLAY MADE EASY 4: Timing and Communication
HOW GOOD IS YOUR BRIDGE HAND?
UNDERSTANDING THE CONTESTED AUCTION
UNDERSTANDING THE UNCONTESTED AUCTION
UNDERSTANDING DUPLICATE PAIRS
UNDERSTANDING SLAM BIDDING

with Hugh Kelsey
NEW INSTANT GUIDE TO BRIDGE

with Mike Lawrence
OPENING LEADS FOR ACOL PLAYERS
OPENING LEADS FLIPPER

with Derek Rimington
IMPROVE YOUR BIDDING AND PLAY

BRIDGE IS FUN

Learn and Laugh with Ron Klinger

Ron Klinger

CASSELL
IN ASSOCIATION WITH
PETER CRAWLEY

First published in Great Britain 2004
in association with Peter Crawley
by Cassell
an imprint of the Orion Publishing Group Ltd
Wellington House, 125 Strand, London WC2R 0BB

© Ron Klinger 2004

The right of Ron Klinger to be identified as the author of
this book has been asserted by him in accordance with
the Copyright, Designs and Patents Act 1988

A catalogue record for this book
is available from the British Library

ISBN 0-304-36668-4

Typeset by Modern Bridge Publications
P.O. Box 140, Northbridge NSW 1560, Australia

Printed and bound in Great Britain by
Clays Ltd, St Ives plc

CONTENTS

Introduction

An apple a day keeps the doctor away? These days there is a better maxim: A good laugh a day keeps the doctor away. Have you noticed that happy, fun-loving people almost never get sick, while the miserable grouches seem to be ill all the time? This is no mere accident. Humour and laughter are genuine healing agents and go hand-in-hand with good health and general well-being.

When you laugh the brain releases endorphins into your body. What, you may ask, are endorphins? This is a chemical compound, which relaxes the body and strengthens the immune system. This in turn will help to defend the body against sickness and so make you live longer. Another option is to have a bridge-playing spouse . . . that may not make you live longer, but it will seem that way.

If you are going to extend your life-span, it will not be enough just to feel good. You will also want to stay mentally agile for as long as you live and that is where bridge comes into the picture. There are countless examples of players in their eighties and nineties not just playing bridge, but also doing particularly well, often winning. The problems in this book aim to raise your game to a higher level in all departments. Make a genuine effort to solve each problem before looking at the complete deal, the solution and the reasoning behind it.

Another rarely touted bonus feature of any bridge book is its sleep-inducing properties. Laugh if you will, but if you are sitting up in bed and pick up a bridge book, no sooner have you started reading than your head will hit the pillow quicker than you can say, 'Making, and redoubled, too'. As one reader was wont to say, 'Once I put down your book, I couldn't pick it up'. Another equally excited reader was given a birthday present, what better than a copy of one of my books, and promptly wrote to thank me: 'I have just received a copy of your latest book. I will waste no time reading it.' Ah, yes, bridge books, the all-natural cure for insomnia.

Another aspect of bridge that cannot be ignored is its wonderful boon to memory. Every day we lose thousands of brain cells, most of which are replenished. The more often you play, the more memory cells are created – some partners will also give you more aggravation cells. According to my calculations, this book by itself, if you do every problem, should restore about 83,147 memory cells, give or take a few thousand. The mathematics of memory cells is not an exact science, you realise.

Here is an unsolicited testimonial from another enthralled reader attesting to the power of bridge for memory:

"You do not know me, but I have read quite a few of your books. I would point out that *Improve Your Bridge Memory* and *Better Bridge With A Better Memory* have not succeeded in one respect! I lent my books out to family or friend and cannot remember who borrowed them. I went to my library in Chichester, West Sussex, to see whether they had a copy, but was told that it was 'missing'. Someone had . . . forgotten to return the book . . . The Librarian was kind enough to check in Surrey, West Sussex and East Sussex, but here again the books were missing. Can you please consider inserting a bookmark in the future to the effect, 'This book was borrowed from . . . who would appreciate its return', to cater for these lapses of memory."

What more can I say? Go. Attack the problems. Step up your endorphin production. Increase your longevity. Add to your memory cells. No, no, no . . . don't start falling asleep already.

Ron Klinger, 2004

PART 1: Improve Your Constructive Bidding
(when the opponents have not entered the auction)

1 Teams : North dealer : Both vulnerable

West	North	East	South
	Pass	Pass	?

What would you do as South with:
- ♠ Q J 6 2
- ♡ Q 10 8 6
- ◇ K Q 10
- ♣ Q 8

2 (a) Teams : West dealer : N-S vulnerable

West	North	East	South
Pass	Pass	1♠	Pass
2♣	Pass	2◇	Pass
3◇	Pass	3♡	Pass
4♣	Pass	4◇	Pass
?			

What would you do as West with:
- ♠ - - -
- ♡ 9 8
- ◇ Q 7 5 4
- ♣ A Q 8 6 5 3 2

2 (b) Teams : West dealer : Both vulnerable

West	North	East	South
1♡	Pass	?	

What would you do as East with:
- ♠ 9
- ♡ K Q 10 4
- ◇ Q 7 6 2
- ♣ K Q J 8

1 Forward Pass

North dealer : Both vulnerable

```
            North
            ♠ 10 8 7
            ♡ K 3 2
            ◇ 8 7 5
            ♣ A K 6 4
West                    East
♠ 5                     ♠ A K 9 4 3
♡ A J 9 5               ♡ 7 4
◇ A 6 3                 ◇ J 9 4 2
♣ J 10 7 3 2            ♣ 9 5
            South
            ♠ Q J 6 2
            ♡ Q 10 8 6
            ◇ K Q 10
            ♣ Q 8
```

In a national teams final:

West	North	East	South
	Pass	Pass	1NT (1)
Pass	Pass	Pass	

(1) 12-14

Opening Lead: ♣3

South won the lead and played a heart to the king, followed by a spade to the queen. The next spade went to the ten and king, West ditching a diamond, and East returned a heart to the ten and jack. West reverted to a top club, won in dummy, and declarer led a heart to the eight and nine. Another high club was won in dummy and a spade was led. East rose with the ♠A, West pitching another diamond, and switched to a diamond. West had the rest of the tricks. Declarer made one spade, one heart and three clubs for two down, −200.

At the other table, the deal was passed in. Full marks to South, who was able to resist opening that rubbish.

Here is an interesting rough guide when considering a light opening: Add your HCP to the number of cards in your two longest suits. Then add your quick tricks (A-K = 2, A-Q = 1½, A = 1, K-Q = 1, K-x = ½). If the answer is 22 or more, open the bidding. Even 21½ is reasonable. Below that, a pass is in order but you can stretch a point at favourable vulnerability.

The South hand has 12 HCP plus 8 (cards in spades and hearts) plus 1 quick trick = 21. Therefore South should pass. A number of useful adjustments can be made to this rough guide (such as deducting a point for singleton K, Q or J).

Pass: A word heard often, but not often enough, at the bridge table.

1 May the fit be with you

West	East
♠ - - -	♠ A K Q 5 4
♡ 9 8	♡ A 7
◇ Q 7 5 4	◇ K 9 6 3
♣ A Q 8 6 5 3 2	♣ J 4

The actual auction:

West	North	East	South
Pass	Pass	1♠	Pass
2♣	Pass	2◇	Pass
3◇	Pass	3♡	Pass
4♣	Pass	4◇	Pass
Pass	Pass		

West might have opened with a pre-empt but having passed, the club length does justify the 2-over-1 response with 8 HCP (expectancy is 10 points or more). 3♡ seeks help in hearts for 3NT. With no values in hearts, West bid 4♣ to show extra length in clubs and also to suggest that the support for diamonds was minimal.

To West, 4◇ sounded like a signoff, perhaps with a 5-2-5-1 pattern. Should East raise 4♣ to 5♣? In my view, yes, and 5♣ is a significantly better game than 5◇.

'Slipstream': The constant flow of errors from partner.

West	East
♠ A 7 6	♠ 9
♡ A 8 7 3 2	♡ K Q 10 4
◇ 9	◇ Q 7 6 2
♣ A 6 5 2	♣ K Q J 8

West	North	East	South
1♡	Pass	3♠	Pass
4♣	Pass	4♡	Pass
5♡	Pass	6♡	All pass

The 3♠ jump was a 'splinter', showing a singleton or void in spades, 4+ hearts and about an opening hand or stronger. It suggests a slam if the fit is good. Despite the minimum opening, West could see slam potential. If East had the high card values for game, the two spade ruffs in dummy could raise the trick tally to twelve.

4♣ showed 1st or 2nd round control in clubs and 4♡ denied 1st and 2nd round control in diamonds. With a sure loser in diamonds, West needed strong trumps opposite. ♡Q-x-x-x would not do. 5♡ said, 'Bid six if your trumps are good', and East obliged. The slam is excellent with just 25 HCP.

'Major fit': Declarer's usual reaction on seeing dummy

3 Playing match-pointed pairs, with your 1NT opening as 15-17, would you choose 1♠ or 1NT with these hands:

(a) In third seat, neither side vulnerable

♠ Q J 7 6 4
♡ K 7 3
♢ A K
♣ Q 10 7

(b) In second seat, both sides vulnerable

♠ Q 10 6 5 4
♡ A 5 2
♢ K 4
♣ A K 7

4 Teams : West dealer : East-West vulnerable

West	North	East	South
Pass	Pass	Pass	?

You are playing a 1NT opening as 15-18. What action would you take as South with:

♠ Q 6 2
♡ A 3
♢ K 8 2
♣ A K Q 7 3

5 Pairs : South dealer : East-West vulnerable

West	North	East	South
			1♣
Pass	1♡	Pass	1♠
Pass	?		

What would you do as North with:

♠ 8
♡ Q 8 7 5 4 2
◇ K 7 5 4 3
♣ A

6 East dealer : Both vulnerable

West	North	East	South
		Pass	1◇
Pass	1♡	Pass	?

What would you do as South with:

♠ 4
♡ K 10 5
◇ K 9 7 6 5
♣ A Q 9 8

14

3 No-trumps suits

3 Can your 1NT opening have a 5-card major? Traditionally, opening 1NT with a 5-3-3-2 was limited to a 5-card minor. Most experts these days allow 1NT with a 5-card major for several reasons. It can keep the bidding lower, allows the stronger hand to be declarer in no-trumps and if no major suit fit exists, you have disclosed less of your hand to the opponents. Both deals are from the final of a major pairs championship. The 1NT was strong, 15-17 points.

```
              North
              ♠ A K 10 5
              ♡ 6 5 4
              ◇ 10 7 5
              ♣ 6 5 4
West                      East
♠ 8 3 2                   ♠ 9
♡ 10 9 8                  ♡ A Q J 2
◇ Q 9 6 3                 ◇ J 8 4 2
♣ A J 2                   ♣ K 9 8 3
              South
              ♠ Q J 7 6 4
              ♡ K 7 3
              ◇ A K
              ♣ Q 10 7
```

West	North	East	South
	Pass	Pass	1NT (1)
Pass	Pass	Pass	

(1) 15-17

Lead: ♡10. Eight tricks +120.

What if South opens 1♠? If North bids 2♠, South passes and makes +110, not as good at pairs as +120. Some might bid to 3♠, a contract that should fail even though ♡A is onside.

West dealer : Both vulnerable

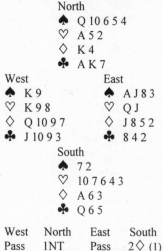

```
              North
              ♠ Q 10 6 5 4
              ♡ A 5 2
              ◇ K 4
              ♣ A K 7
West                      East
♠ K 9                     ♠ A J 8 3
♡ K 9 8                   ♡ Q J
◇ Q 10 9 7                ◇ J 8 5 2
♣ J 10 9 3                ♣ 8 4 2
              South
              ♠ 7 2
              ♡ 10 7 6 4 3
              ◇ A 6 3
              ♣ Q 6 5
```

West	North	East	South
Pass	1NT	Pass	2◇ (1)
Pass	2♡	All pass	

(1) Transfer to hearts

Declarer made 9 tricks, losing 2 spades and 2 hearts. If North opens 1♠ South replies 1NT and North might raise to 2NT, which South should pass. Note that the heart suit has been lost. +140 is available in hearts, but only +90 or +120 in 1NT/2NT.

4 Cool Kalmin Collected

Lynn Kalmin produced a fine play on this deal from a major teams championship:

West dealer : Nil vulnerable

```
              North
              ♠ 9 7 3
              ♡ K Q 7 4
              ◇ Q 10
              ♣ 10 8 6 2
West                        East
♠ A K J 10                  ♠ 8 5 4
♡ 10 8 6 5 2                ♡ J 9
◇ J 7 3                     ◇ A 9 6 5 4
♣ 9                         ♣ J 5 4
              South
              Lynn Kalmin
              ♠ Q 6 2
              ♡ A 3
              ◇ K 8 2
              ♣ A K Q 7 3
```

West	North	East	South
Pass	Pass	Pass	1♣
Dble	1♡	Pass	2NT
Pass	3NT	All pass	

Lead: ♠K

If your 1NT opening is 15-18 or 16-18, South is too good for 1NT. Upgrade a hand by one point for a 5-card suit. That makes the South hand worth 19 points and bid it as such. Open 1♣ and the jump-rebid in no-trumps will show your strength.

On the ♠K lead, East played the ♠4, discouraging. To defeat 3NT West needs to switch to a diamond. East wins and returns a spade. Not clairvoyant, West switched to a low heart at trick 2.

Kalmin won with the ace and played off the ♣A, ♣K, ♣Q, unblocking dummy's ♣10, ♣8. West discarded a heart and a diamond. On the ♣7, West discarded another diamond.

This was now the position:

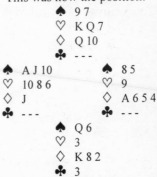

```
              ♠ 9 7
              ♡ K Q 7
              ◇ Q 10
              ♣ - - -
♠ A J 10            ♠ 8 5
♡ 10 8 6            ♡ 9
◇ J                 ◇ A 6 5 4
♣ - - -            ♣ - - -
              ♠ Q 6
              ♡ 3
              ◇ K 8 2
              ♣ 3
```

On the ♣3 West pitched the ◇J. Kalmin now played ♡K, ♡Q and put West on lead with the fourth heart, leaving herself with ♠Q-6 and ◇K. She now made the ♠Q for +400, with the datum (average) N-S 100.

'Opponents': the other 3 players.

5 Department of the Inferior

When we first learn this game, the answers in class are usually clear-cut. When we start playing, there seem to be so many choices. The task then is to choose the best option, with the heavy emphasis on not bidding too little with a strong hand or too much with a poor hand. This deal from a casual duplicate is a good example of the latter error.

South dealer : E-W vulnerable

```
              North
              ♠ 8
              ♡ Q 8 7 5 4 2
              ◇ K 7 5 4 3
              ♣ A
West                      East
♠ A 9 3 2                 ♠ J 7 6 5
♡ K J 9                   ♡ A 3
◇ J 10 6                  ◇ Q 9 8 2
♣ 9 8 7                   ♣ K 10 4
              South
              ♠ K Q 10 4
              ♡ 10 6
              ◇ A
              ♣ Q J 6 5 3 2
```

West	North	East	South
			1♣
Pass	1♡	Pass	1♠
Pass	2◇	Pass	3♣
Pass	Pass	Pass	

Lead: ◇J

South won the lead and played a club to the ace to discard a heart on the ◇K. Then came the ♠8 to declarer's ten and the ace. West continued with the third diamond, ruffed by declarer.

The ♣Q went to the king and the ◇Q now created an extra trump trick for the defence. Declarer still had a spade to lose and went one down, −50, losing two spades, one heart and two clubs.

North did too much with the 2◇ bid, which is forcing (forcing to game for many pairs). North should rebid 2♡ to slow the auction down. With a minimum, South should pass 2♡ and on most lines of play, declarer can make eight tricks.

Understanding bridge jargon:
'Missed the obvious line . . .' = The writer is hostile towards the declarer who failed to find a triple transfer guard squeeze.

'Beaten by an unlucky lie of the cards . . .' = The writer is a good friend of the declarer who went two down in a laydown contract.

6 Raising Cain

Failure to adhere to basic bidding cost a game on this deal from the final of a major teams championship:

East dealer : Both vulnerable

```
           North
           ♠ K J 9
           ♡ A 8 6 4 2
           ◇ Q J 10 3
           ♣ 7
West                    East
♠ A 8 7 5 2            ♠ Q 10 6 3
♡ 9 7 3               ♡ Q J
◇ A 8                ◇ 4 2
♣ K 5 2              ♣ J 10 6 4 3
           South
           ♠ 4
           ♡ K 10 5
           ◇ K 9 7 6 5
           ♣ A Q 9 8
```

West	North	East	South
		Pass	1◇
1♠	2♡	2♠ (1)	4♡
Pass	Pass	Pass	

(1) A pre-emptive 3♠ appeals.

Declarer made ten tricks for +620. At the other table:

West	North	East	South
		Pass	1◇
Pass	1♡	Pass	2♣??
Pass	3◇	All pass	

Lead: ♠A

Declarer lost a spade and a diamond, +150 but −10 Imps.

South has an automatic raise to 2♡ (instead of 2♣) and North will then jump to 4♡ to tie the board. Many experts would raise responder's major to the two-level with three-card support even with a 4-4-3-2 or 5-3-3-2 pattern. With a singleton outside, the single raise with 3-card support is clear-cut.

After 1◇ : 1♡, opener has no attractive direct raise with a hand like this:

```
♠ 4
♡ K 10 5
◇ K J 7 6 5
♣ A K Q 8
```

and a 2♣ rebid is warranted. The hand is too strong for a single raise and a jump-raise (1◇ : 1♡, 3♡) promises four trumps in support.

"What do you think of my game?"
"I like it, but I still prefer bridge."

'Tis not whether you win or lose, but how you place the blame.

The best gift you can give your bridge partner: A good example.

7   West dealer : Nil vulnerable

West	North	East	South
Pass	Pass	Pass	2♣
Pass	2NT	Pass	3♠
Pass	?		

What would you do as North with:

♠ Q 4 3
♡ A 7
♢ K 7 6 5
♣ 10 6 3 2

8   South dealer : East-West vulnerable

West	North	East	South
			1♠
Pass	2♣	Pass	3♠
Pass	?		

What would you do as North with:

♠ 7 3
♡ A K 10 5
♢ 9 8 7
♣ A Q 4 2

9 North dealer : East-West vulnerable

West	North	East	South
	1♡	Pass	1♠
Pass	2♡	Pass	?

What action would you take as South with:

♠ A K 8 6
♡ A J 9
◇ A 8 3 2
♣ 9 7

10 South dealer : East-West vulnerable

West	North	East	South
			1♠
Pass	2♣	Pass	2◇
Pass	2♡ (1)	Pass	3◇
Pass	3♠	Pass	?

(1) Fourth-suit forcing to game

What would you do now as South with:

♠ K J 9 7 5
♡ A 10 9
◇ A Q J 10 2
♣ - - -

7 Perry good bidding

This deal arose in a major selection tournament:

West dealer : Nil vulnerable

```
              North
              Neil Perry
              ♠ Q 4 3
              ♡ A 7
              ◇ K 7 6 5
              ♣ 10 6 3 2
West                        East
♠ 8 7                       ♠ 9 2
♡ 9 6 5 3                   ♡ Q J 10 8 4 2
◇ 4 3 2                     ◇ J 9 8
♣ K Q J 5                   ♣ 7 4
              South
              Peter Jamieson
              ♠ A K J 10 6 5
              ♡ K
              ◇ A Q 10
              ♣ A 9 8
```

West	North	East	South
Pass	Pass	Pass	2♣ (1)
Pass	2NT (2)	Pass	3♠
Pass	4◇	Pass	6♠
Pass	Pass	Pass	

(1) Game force or 23+ HCP
(2) Usually balanced with about 7-9 points

After Jamieson showed 5+ spades with the 3♠ rebid, Perry found the good cue-bid of 4◇, showing spade support, first- or second-round control in diamonds and denying first- or second-round control in clubs. That was sufficient for Jamieson to jump to 6♠, as North would probably have simply raised to 4♠ with the ◇K and no other control card. Still, it would not have hurt to bid 4NT to ask for key cards.

All thirteen tricks were made, +1010. That was worth +11 Imps against the median score of +510. Had East chosen a 3♡ opening or a weak 2♡ in third seat, it would be much harder for North-South to find the slam.

Happiness: 6NT making seven.
Misery: 7NT making six.

Judgement: Impeccable if by you, poor when attempted by partner.

Fortune favours the brave but turns her back on the suicidal.

Understanding bridge jargon:

'Failed to take a safety play' = Blunder committed by a novice

'Missed the best line' = The same play by a strong player

'Took the wrong view' = The same play by an expert

8 Slam Dunk

In events scored by Imps, accurate slam bidding is essential. At pairs, a slam rates as much as any other board but at teams, missing a good slam or failing in a bad one can be very costly. This deal arose in a national selection event:

South dealer : E-W vulnerable

```
              North
              ♠ 7 3
              ♡ A K 10 5
              ◊ 9 8 7
              ♣ A Q 4 2
West                      East
♠ J 10 9                  ♠ 8 6
♡ J 4                     ♡ 9 7 3 2
◊ Q 10 6 3                ◊ A J 5 2
♣ J 10 9 6                ♣ 7 5 3
              South
              ♠ A K Q 5 4 2
              ♡ Q 8 6
              ◊ K 4
              ♣ K 8
```

West	North	East	South
			1♠
Pass	2♣	Pass	3♠
Pass	4♡ (1)	Pass	4NT
Pass	5♡	Pass	6♠
Pass	Pass	Pass	

(1) Cue-bid, showing support for spades and slam interest

Over 3♠, the 'easy', lazy bid is 4♠, but North should do more than this. This is a good guide for judging your hand: opening hand + opening hand = game; opening hand opposite opener who makes a jump rebid = slam potential if a trump fit exists.

If you are not prepared to bid 4NT as North, then you should at least make a cue-bid of 4♡ to show spade support and a top card in hearts. This is more useful than to reserve 4♡ for a freakish hand with six clubs and five hearts.

The small slam in spades is excellent, depending on little more than a 3-2 trump break. Scoring was by Imps against every other score. In both the open and the women's section, three pairs bid 6♠ (+50 Imps) and five stopped in game (minus 30 Imps).

'Convention': A scientific way of reaching the wrong contract

'Protesting the Director's ruling':
An unjustifiable objection by the opponents to a fair ruling by the Director or a fair objection by you to an unjustifiable ruling by the Director.

9 Aim higher

On this deal from a national open teams championship only a handful of pairs found the excellent 6♡:

North dealer : E-W vulnerable

```
                North
                ♠ 10 9 7
                ♡ K Q 8 6 5 4
                ◇ K 10 5
                ♣ A
West                        East
♠ J                         ♠ Q 5 4 3 2
♡ 7 2                       ♡ 10 3
◇ 7 6 4                     ◇ Q J 9
♣ K 10 8 6 4 3 2           ♣ Q J 5
                South
                ♠ A K 8 6
                ♡ A J 9
                ◇ A 8 3 2
                ♣ 9 7
```

West	North	East	South
	1♡	Pass	1♠
Pass	2♡	Pass	3◇
Pass	3♠	Pass	4♡
Pass	4NT (1)	Pass	5◇ (2)
Pass	5♡ (3)	Pass	6♡
Pass	Pass	Pass	

(1) Roman Key-Card Blackwood
(2) One or four key cards
(3) In case it is only one

Whether North tackles the diamonds or the spades, 6♡ will succeed. After 1♡ : 1♠,

2♡ you must not give slam away by signing off in 4♡. There are so many hands where 6♡ is laydown without much skill required in declarer play. Give North the same trumps and ♣A-K-x or just the ♠Q-J instead of the ◇K. Even 7♡ is not out of the question. Give North QJ / KQxxxxx / xx / Ax.

South needs to make some slam effort over 2♡ and a forcing 3◇ is best. When North reverts to 3♠, South bids 4♡, showing slam interest but club weakness.

In the olden days, this would show a singleton in clubs and a 5-3-4-1 pattern. Nowadays, South would make a splinter-jump to 4♣ over 2♡ to show a club singleton. Thus the given sequence should show slam interest but deny a singleton.

'Reverse': When partner takes a bid to have the opposite meaning of the one you intended.

Short club: Prelude in A Minor

JFK rule: 'Ask not what your partner can do for you; ask what you can do for yourself.'

10 Slammed shut

In the final of a national open teams championship, the margin was just 1 Imp. The winners had a considerable slice of luck when they bid and made slam on this deal:

South dealer : E-W vulnerable

```
              North
              ♠ A 2
              ♥ J 7 6
              ♦ 4 3
              ♣ A K 10 9 7 5

West                      East
♠ 10 6 3                  ♠ Q 8 4
♥ K Q                     ♥ 8 5 4 3 2
♦ 9 8 7 6                 ♦ K 5
♣ Q 4 3 2                 ♣ J 8 6

              South
              ♠ K J 9 7 5
              ♥ A 10 9
              ♦ A Q J 10 2
              ♣ - - -
```

West	North	East	South
			1♠
Pass	2♣	Pass	2♦
Pass	2♥ (1)	Pass	3♦
Pass	3♠	Pass	?

(1) Fourth-suit forcing to game

At one table South had bid 4♠ over 3♦. North bid 4NT and then 6♠ over the 5♥ reply.

At the other table South bid 4♥ (cue-bid) over 3♠ and North signed off in 4♠. The best bid over 3♠ is 3NT but how can you deduce that?

Partnerships would do well to discuss the meaning of 3♠ and 4♠ after the 3♦ rebid. Does 3♠ promise three-card support with slam interest or can it be a doubleton, angling for the best spot (in which case South should rebid 3NT)? If a 2-over-1 response followed by a jump-bid is forcing to game, then 3♠ over 2♦ would show the strong hand with 3-card support and slam interest. In that case the 4th-suit sequence followed by 3♠ shows two spades only and expresses doubt as to the best contract.

This is a hideous slam but it made, thanks to the 3-3 trump split with the ♠Q onside, plus diamonds no worse than 4-2. Chances in toto: about 15%.

In toto: How Dorothy called her dog home.

'It is good to make one person happy each day . . . try not to choose your opponent at bridge as that person.'

11   South dealer : Both vulnerable

West	North	East	South
			1♠ (1)
Pass	?		

(1) Playing 5-card majors

What would you do as North with:

♠ 6 4 3 2
♡ 8 6 5
♢ A Q J 9 8 6
♣ - - -

12   South dealer : Nil vulnerable

West	North	East	South
			1♡
Pass	3♠ (1)	Pass	?

(1) Splinter game-raise, 4+ hearts, shortage in spades

What would you rebid as South with:

♠ A 10 7 6
♡ Q 10 8 6 4 2
♢ 5
♣ A 7

13   West dealer : East-West vulnerable

West	North	East	South
Pass	1♣ (1)	Pass	1♠
Pass	4♣ (2)	Pass	?

(1) 15+ points, any shape
(2) Splinter raise, 4+ spades, short clubs

What action would you take as South with:

♠ Q J 7 6 5
♡ 10 4
◇ Q J 2
♣ A K 4

14   North dealer : Both vulnerable

West	North	East	South
	1♠	Pass	2♡
Pass	4♣ (1)	Pass	?

(1) Splinter, 4+ hearts, singleton or void in clubs

What would you do now as South with:

♠ A 7
♡ K Q 9 8 7 5
◇ - - -
♣ A K J 10 2

11 A ruff splinter

This deal arose in a major selection pairs tournament, with Imp scoring:

South dealer : Both vulnerable

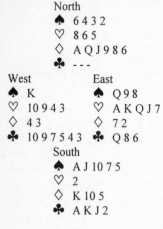

North
♠ 6 4 3 2
♡ 8 6 5
♦ A Q J 9 8 6
♣ - - -

West
♠ K
♡ 10 9 4 3
♦ 4 3
♣ 10 9 7 5 4 3

East
♠ Q 9 8
♡ A K Q J 7
♦ 7 2
♣ Q 8 6

South
♠ A J 10 7 5
♡ 2
♦ K 10 5
♣ A K J 2

North	South
	1♠
4♣ (1)	4NT (2)
5♦ (3)	5♠
Pass	

(1) Splinter, short in clubs
(2) RKCB
(3) 1 or 4 key-cards, clearly one

Slam may not be a good bet, but that does not mean it will fail. Witness:

South	North
Alan Walsh	*Ted Chadwick*
1♠	3♦ (1)
4♡ (2)	6♦ (3)
6♠	Pass

(1) 10-12 points, 4+ spades
(2) Splinter, short in hearts
(3) Choice of 6♦ or 6♠

After 1♠ : Pass, North has a tough problem. The hand has only 7 HCP but excellent playing strength with a void, a strong side suit and only seven losers. One might jump to 4♠ but that virtually gives up any hope of slam. As it happens, slam is not a good proposition but give South the ♡A singleton and worthless clubs and slam is a strong chance.

This is a possible auction:

A heart lead would of course spell doom but in view of South's splinter in hearts, West chose the ♣10. Away went dummy's three hearts on South's clubs. Then came ♠A, felling the king, followed by the ♠J. Declarer won the return, drew the missing trump, ruffed his heart loser in dummy for effect and claimed.

'I splintered,' Walsh said later, 'but dummy scored the heart ruff.'

12 True Lies

Giving a wrong response to Roman Key-Card Blackwood is not recommended but there are circumstances which dictate such an approach.

What is more important, strength or shape? This deal is testimony to the power of shape:

South dealer : Nil vulnerable

```
              North
              ♠ Q
              ♡ K 9 7 5 3
              ◇ A K 10 3
              ♣ 9 6 4
West                      East
♠ K 8 5 4                 ♠ J 9 3 2
♡ A J                     ♡ - - -
◇ Q 9 7 4                 ◇ J 8 6 2
♣ J 5 2                   ♣ K Q 10 8 3
              South
              ♠ A 10 7 6
              ♡ Q 10 8 6 4 2
              ◇ 5
              ♣ A 7
```

West	North	East	South
			1♡
Pass	3♠ (1)	Pass	4NT (2)
Pass	5♠ (3)	Pass	6♡
Pass	Pass	Pass	

(1) Splinter game-raise, 4+ hearts, shortage in spades
(2) Roman Key-Card Blackwood
(3) Two key-cards + the ♡Q

4NT was well-judged. With first- or second-round control in every suit outside trumps, there was no need to make a cue-bid. As long as North had two or three key-cards, slam was likely to be a good bet despite South's minimum opening.

In reply to 4NT, North showed the ♡Q although he did not hold it. As North-South were playing 5-card majors, North's five trumps were almost as valuable as having the trump queen. With A-x-x-x-x opposite K-x-x-x-x, the chance of no loser is 78%. This improves to 89% with A-J-x-x-x opposite K-x-x-x-x as long as you play the king first. An extra chance is a 6-card suit with opener.
Principle: If your side has ten or more trumps, include the trump queen in reply to a Roman Key-Card Ask.

There was no problem in the play. With the ♠Q wasted, the power of shape makes the slam easy with only 20 useful HCP between the two hands.

'Splinter': A thorn in the side that uses it

13 Patronising Comments

Australia (Ishmael Del'Monte – Paul Marston, George Gaspar – Bob Richman) led their section at the end of Day 2 of the Commonwealth Nations Bridge Championships. The win against Patron 1 was particularly satisfying as it contained a strong English squad (John Armstrong – Tony Forrester, Jason Hackett – Justin Hackett – Paul Hackett). On this deal Australia outbid Patron 1 to reach an excellent slam:

West dealer : E-W vulnerable

```
            North
            ♠ A 10 9 8 3
            ♡ A K 9 2
            ◇ A 7 5
            ♣ 3
West                    East
♠ 4                     ♠ K 2
♡ 8 7 6 5               ♡ Q J 3
◇ K 10 8 6              ◇ 9 4 3
♣ Q J 8 5              ♣ 10 9 7 6 2
            South
            ♠ Q J 7 6 5
            ♡ 10 4
            ◇ Q J 2
            ♣ A K 4
```

With East-West silent, Patron 1 had an uninspiring 1♠ : 3NT, 4♣ : 4♠ sequence. At the other table:

West	North	East	South
	Richman		*Gaspar*
Pass	1♣ (1)	Pass	1♠
Pass	4♣ (2)	Pass	4NT
Pass	5♣ (3)	Pass	6♠
Pass	Pass	Pass	

(1) 15+ points, any shape
(2) Splinter raise, 4+ spades, singleton or void in clubs
(3) 0 or 3 key-cards, clearly 3

The Daily Bulletin took a jibe at South's use of 4NT here with both red suits unguarded. What else was South to do if interested in slam? In fact the ♣K was useful for a diamond discard and South has more than a minimum response.

Given North's expected strength it was highly likely that both red suits were controlled. The practical approach was to use 4NT to ensure that two key-cards were not missing. The Bulletin editors might have done better to examine the inept bidding at the other table. Twelve tricks were routine for +980 and 11 Imps to Australia.

Relay system: A modern, scientific method of reaching the wrong contract in which only one player gets the blame.

14 The Force Is Grand

After 4NT for aces or key cards, 5NT asks for kings. A 5NT bid without using 4NT first is a Trump Ask, often known as the Grand Slam Force. 5NT asks, 'How many of the top three trumps (A, K and Q) do you have?'

There are various versions of replies. Since it comes up rarely, a simple structure is best. One possibility: 6♣ = 0, 6♦ = 1, 6♥ = 2, 6♠ = 3. A slightly more sophisticated version: Bid the agreed trump suit with none. Otherwise, cheapest bid = 1, next bid = A + K, next bid = K-Q or A-Q and bid seven with all three.

The Grand Slam Force would find the grand slam on this deal *(see next column)* from a national Imp pairs event:

West	North	East	South
	1♠	Pass	2♥
Pass	4♣ (1)	Pass	5NT (2)
Pass	6♣ (3)	Pass	7♥
Pass	Pass	Pass	

(1) Splinter raise, 4+ hearts, singleton or void in clubs
(2) Trump Ask
(3) One top honour in hearts

North dealer : Both vulnerable

```
            North
            ♠ K Q 10 9 2
            ♥ A 6 3 2
            ♦ Q 9 5
            ♣ 5
West                    East
♠ J                     ♠ 8 6 5 4 3
♥ J 4                   ♥ 10
♦ K 10 7 6 4 2          ♦ A J 8 3
♣ Q 9 6 4               ♣ 8 7 3
            South
            ♠ A 7
            ♥ K Q 9 8 7 5
            ♦ - - -
            ♣ A K J 10 2
```

On learning that North has one top trump honour, South should bid 7♥. Having opened the bidding, North will have sufficient values to take care of the potential loser in spades.

Of 42 North-South pairs, only three bid the grand slam. That was worth 13 Imps as the datum (average) was N-S 1420.

The 5NT Asking Convention
5NT says 'How much of the early bidding did you get right?'
The answers start with:
6♣: *'Hopeless. I was lost from the outset'.*
6♦: *'The first couple of bids were OK, but it was shaky after that.'*

PART 2: Improve Your Competitive Bidding

15   Teams : North dealer : Nil vulnerable

West	North	East	South
	Pass	Pass	1♡ (1)
Dble	2♡	Dble (2)	?

(1) Playing 5-card majors
(2) Responsive double, shows both minors

What would you do as South with:

♠ J
♡ Q J 10 8 4
♢ A 10
♣ Q 10 6 4 2

16   Teams : East dealer : Both vulnerable

West	North	East	South
		Pass	Pass
1♠	Dble	2♠	?

What would you do as South with:

♠ 8
♡ K J 9 3 2
♢ A 8 4 3
♣ 10 8 7

17 Teams : West dealer : Nil vulnerable

West	North	East	South
2♡ (1)	Pass	Pass	Dble (2)
Pass	Pass (3)	3♣	Dble (3)
?			

(1) Multi-2♡, weak hand with 5+ hearts and a 4+ minor
(2) Takeout double
(3) For penalties

What would you do as West with:

♠ K 10 4
♡ A 10 8 6 2
♢ J 10 9 7 3
♣ - - -

18 Pairs : West dealer : East-West vulnerable

West	North	East	South
Pass (1)	1♢	Dble	1♠
?			

(1) Not playing weak twos

What would you do as West with:

♠ K Q 9 8 4 3
♡ J 4
♢ 10 5 2
♣ 6 3

15 'And somewhere hearts are light'

This deal from the final of a teams championship featured a light opening bid:

North dealer : Nil vulnerable

          North
          ♠ A Q 9 8 6
          ♡ 6 5 3
          ◇ J 9 4
          ♣ 7 3
West   East
♠ 5 4 3 2   ♠ K 10 7
♡ K 9 2   ♡ A 7
◇ K Q 8 7   ◇ 6 5 3 2
♣ A J   ♣ K 9 8 5
          South
          ♠ J
          ♡ Q J 10 8 4
          ◇ A 10
          ♣ Q 10 6 4 2

West	North	East	South
	Pass	Pass	1♡
Dble	2♡	Dble (1)	3♡
Pass	Pass	Dble	All pass

(1) Responsive double, both minors

Lead: ◇K

West's takeout double, with length in opener's suit and lack of tolerance in an unbid suit, is no thing of beauty with such minimum values. Still, it worked a treat here when she elected to pass East's competitive double of 3♡.

Opening light is one thing. Bidding again opposite a weak hand with 3-card support is another. South paid quite a price for competing to the 3-level. The ◇K lead was taken by the ace. Declarer led the ♠J and overtook with dummy's queen. East won and exited with the ♡7 to the queen, king, and West returned a spade won by the ace, on which South ditched the ◇10.

Declarer now led a club to the 10 and jack and West returned a heart to East's ace. The diamond shift was ruffed by declarer, who played another club, won by the ace. West exited with her third heart, won by declarer, who led another club to East. A diamond now removed declarer's last trump with the clubs not yet established. The result was four down for +800 and +12 Imps when East-West scored --150 at the other table.

Bridge player: One who calls a spade two spades.

Bidding box: A device to prevent you making your errors orally

16 Slow White & The Seven Imps

The scene: A national teams championship in Australia. One of the experts is David White, Professor of Microbiology. David, who has been near the top of national bridge events for over thirty years, is not renowned for his speedy play.

During the second round match, one of David's opponents calls: 'DIRECTOR!'
Tournament Director David Anderson comes to the table:
Opponent: 'Could you please hurry Professor White up. He is very slow.'
David Anderson: 'If I could hurry Professor White up, I would consider that a Lifetime Achievement Award.'

This deal is from that match:
(see next column)

West	North	East	South
		Pass	Pass
1♠	Dble	2♠	3♡
Pass	Pass	Pass	

3♡ is enough on the South cards. A jump to 4♡ may well goad West into 4♠ and then you have to decide whether to defend or bid on to 5♡.

East dealer : Both vulnerable

```
            North
            ♠ 9 4
            ♡ A Q 6 4
            ◇ K Q 6
            ♣ K 9 5 3
West                     East
♠ A K Q J 10 5           ♠ 7 6 3 2
♡ 10 8 7                 ♡ 5
◇ 10 9 2                 ◇ J 7 5
♣ Q                      ♣ A J 6 4 2
            South
            David White
            ♠ 8
            ♡ K J 9 3 2
            ◇ A 8 4 3
            ♣ 10 8 7
```

If North raises 3♡ to 4♡, the opponents may be less inclined to sacrifice in 4♠ because of your slower auction. If North passes 3♡, then perhaps 4♡ might not make.

Although the defence can come to four tricks, White made ten tricks and wrote +170 into his score-book. He was satisfied when the result from the other table came in: 5♡, one down, +100. That was worth 7 Imps.

Bridge columnist: Jack of all tirades

17 Indiscreet

This deal arose in a national teams championship:

West dealer : Nil vulnerable

```
            North
            ♠ 9 7 5
            ♡ K Q J 9 5
            ◇ 8 5
            ♣ K 7 4
West                    East
♠ K 10 4                ♠ 6 3 2
♡ A 10 8 6 2            ♡ 4 3
◇ J 10 9 7 3           ◇ 6 4
♣ - - -                 ♣ A Q J 10 9 8
            South
            ♠ A Q J 8
            ♡ 7
            ◇ A K Q 2
            ♣ 6 5 3 2
```

West	North	East	South
2♡(1)	Pass	Pass	Dble (2)
Pass	Pass (3)	3♣	Dble (3)
3◇	Dble (3)	All pass	

(1) Multi-2♡, weak hand with 5+ hearts and a 4+ minor
(2) Takeout double
(3) For penalties

West should pass 3♣ doubled. East has not sought your opinion, therefore leave 3♣ alone. To locate West's minor, East could have run to 2♠ or to 2NT and then redoubled, asking for rescue.

Another sound treatment in the given auction is for East to redouble, saying 'Please make the cheapest bid and then pass my next bid.' East would redouble 2♡, West would bid 2♠ and East's 3♣ must then be passed. (Clearly it is important that both partners are aware of this use of redouble.)

The cost in 3♣ doubled would be 300. It was much more in 3◇ doubled. North led a trump, won by the ◇Q. South shifted to the ♠A, then ♠Q, won by the king. West led a low heart won by South who cashed the ♠J, ◇A and followed with the ♠8. West discarded a heart.

South continued with the ◇K and the ◇2 to keep declarer in hand. West made just two diamond tricks, the ♠K and the ♡A, five down, minus 1100.

'Indiscretion': A term applied to your inferior choice, which would be labelled a blunder if committed by partner.

'Bidding System': A collection of agreements and conventions, which enable two players to reach the wrong contract.

18 Don't go psycho after a psyche

North-South failed to cope with a baby psyche on this deal from a club duplicate:

West dealer : E-W vulnerable

```
                North
                ♠ J 6
                ♡ K 9 5
                ◇ K J 7 4
                ♣ K Q J 9
West                        East
♠ K Q 9 8 4 3               ♠ A 7 5
♡ J 4                       ♡ A Q 6 2
◇ 10 5 2                    ◇ A Q 9
♣ 6 3                       ♣ A 8 4
                South
                ♠ 10 2
                ♡ 10 8 7 3
                ◇ 8 6 3
                ♣ 10 7 5 2
```

West	North	East	South
Pass	1◇	Dble	1♠
Pass	1NT	Dble	2◇
2♠	Pass	2NT	All pass

South psyched 1♠ because of the favourable vulnerability. It is called a 'baby psyche' because it is such a common situation to psyche that only babies are fooled. Both East and West could have done more but in practice languished in a part-score.

After an auction like (1♣ or 1◇) : Double : (1♡ or 1♠), it is best to use a penalty double to expose the psyche. The double says, 'I was going to bid that suit.' You do not need a negative double here. If you have the other major, just bid it. The auction might then go:

West	North	East	South
Pass	1◇	Dble	1♠
Dble	1NT	Dble	2◇
2♠	Pass	4♣	All pass

Here is another psyche, this time from a national teams event:

West dealer : N-S vulnerable

West	North	East	South
Pass	Pass	2◇	Dble
Pass	2♠	Pass	3NT
Pass	Pass	Pass	

N-S were cold for 7NT and East had opened a weak 2◇ on

```
♠ 5 3
♡ 9 8 7 4
◇ J 10 5 2
♣ 9 6 5
```

'Psyche': A brilliancy when committed by you, an idiocy when committed by your team-mates and unethical and unsporting when committed by an opponent.

19   South dealer : Both vulnerable

West	North	East	South
			2♣ (1)
Dble (2)	4♠ (3)	?	

(1) Acol Two
(2) For takeout
(3) Weak raise

What would you do as East with:

♠ K 8 3
♡ Q 10 9
◇ A K
♣ K 9 7 5 2

20   West dealer : North-South vulnerable

West	North	East	South
1♣	2♠	Dble (1)	Pass
?			

(1) For takeout, promises 4+ hearts

What should West do with:

♠ 2
♡ 10 4
◇ A K 5 4
♣ A K Q 10 5 3

21 West dealer : Nil vulnerable

West	North	East	South
Pass	1♣	2◇ (1)	Dble (2)
4◇ (3)	?		

(1) Intermediate jump-overcall
(2) For takeout, shows both majors
(3) Pre-emptive

What action would you take as North with:

♠ K 10 5
♡ A J 8
◇ 3
♣ K Q 10 8 7 4

22 East dealer : Both vulnerable

West	North	East	South
		Pass	1◇
?			

What would you do as West with:

♠ Q 10 9
♡ K J 9
◇ K
♣ A Q 9 7 5 3

19 Swings and roundabouts

This deal arose in the final of a national teams championship:

South dealer : Both vulnerable

```
              North
              ♠  10 9 7
              ♡  8 4 3 2
              ◇  9 8 4 3 2
              ♣  8
West                        East
♠  - - -                    ♠  K 8 3
♡  J 7 6 5                  ♡  Q 10 9
◇  Q J 6 5                  ◇  A K
♣  A Q J 10 4               ♣  K 9 7 5 2
              South
              ♠  A Q J 6 5 4 2
              ♡  A K
              ◇  10 7
              ♣  6 3
```

West	North	East	South
			2♠ (1)
Dble (2)	4♠ (3)	Dble	All pass

(1) Acol Two
(2) For takeout
(3) Weak raise

Perhaps East was thinking, 'Partner has made a takeout double and here I am with 15 points and strong defensive prospects. It does not get much better than this.'

These hopes were soon dashed. West led a heart and declarer played a club at trick 2. West won and shifted to a low diamond. East took this and switched to a trump. Declarer ducked and, after ruffing a club in dummy, was soon writing +790 in his scorebook.

Was East's double unlucky or ill-judged? It was at the very least a touch naive. West figured to have at least 9-10 points. That gives East-West at least 24 HCP. How could North-South be bidding to game when vulnerable with 16 points or less? The answer must be excellent shape to compensate for the lack of high card strength. So it proved, with N-S reaching an unbeatable game with just 14 HCP.

As West was sure to be short in spades, East could expect West to have at least three clubs and probably more. East should bid 5♣, which cannot be beaten as the cards lie.

'Acol Two': A one-opening seen through rose-tinted glasses.

Screen: Device used in major tournaments so that one need no longer keep a straight face on seeing partner's bid.

20 Take me out to the best game

This deal comes from the qualifying rounds of a major teams championship:

West dealer : N-S vulnerable

```
            North
            ♠ A Q J 10 8 6 3
            ♡ K 7
            ◇ Q 9 7
            ♣ 9
West                    East
♠ 2                     ♠ K 4
♡ 10 4                  ♡ Q J 9 6 3
◇ A K 5 4               ◇ J 10 6 2
♣ A K Q 10 5 3          ♣ J 7
            South
            ♠ 9 7 5
            ♡ A 8 5 2
            ◇ 8 3
            ♣ 8 6 4 2
```

At one table the bidding went:

West	North	East	South
1♣	2♠	Dble (1)	Pass
3◇	Pass	4◇	Pass
4NT	Pass	5♣	Pass
5◇	Pass	Pass	Pass

(1) For takeout with 4+ hearts

This went three down after ♠A, ♡K, heart to the ace, third heart ruffed by North and a losing diamond finesse later.

With a likely eight tricks in hand, West should bid 3♠ in response to East's double. This asks East to bid 3NT with a stopper in spades. East has the stopper and 3NT is unbeatable. That is what happened at the other table:

West	North	East	South
1♣	1♠	Dble (1)	Pass
3♠ (2)	Pass	3NT	All pass

(1) Takeout, promises 4+ hearts
(2) Asking partner to bid 3NT with a spade stopper

After East's negative double, West had no hesitation bidding 3♠ to look for the 3NT game. Nine tricks were easy, +400 and +11 Imps.

Understanding bridge journalese:

'Capable of improvement' = 'Incapable of improvement'

* . . . followed by Ed. at the end = footnote containing erudite clarification or a witty riposte.

* . . . followed by the writer's initials = footnote containing unnecessary amplification or feeble attempt at humour.

'It is clear that much additional work will be needed on this relay system before a complete understanding . . .' = 'I don't understand it.'

21 Double can quadruple your options

This deal arose in a Butler Pairs Selection tournament:

West dealer : Nil vulnerable

```
              North
              ♠ K 10 5
              ♡ A J 8
              ◇ 3
              ♣ K Q 10 8 7 4
West                      East
♠ A Q                     ♠ 6 4 2
♡ Q 2                     ♡ 10 5
◇ J 8 7 5 4               ◇ A K Q 10 9
♣ J 9 5 3                 ♣ A 6 2
              South
              ♠ J 9 8 7 3
              ♡ K 9 7 6 4 3
              ◇ 6 2
              ♣ - - -
```

West	North	East	South
Pass	1♣	2◇	Dble
4◇	5♣	All pass	

The 2◇ jump-overcall was intermediate (about 11-15 HCP and a 6+ suit). South's double showed both majors and West's jump to 4◇ was pre-emptive. A good guide for competitive bidding: 'With ten trumps bid for at least ten tricks.' At favourable vulnerability, West would be entitled to jump to 5◇.

North's 5♣ bid was insensitive and he paid the price. 5♣ failed miserably while eleven tricks are there in either major.

To bid 5♣ is to put all your eggs in one basket. *Sensible rule: If the opponents bid and raise a suit immediately, double is for takeout.* North should have doubled 4◇ for takeout. Consider not what you hold but what the partnership may have.

Bidding 5♣ can have only one good outcome, but doubling gives you four chances of success: 4♡, 4♠, 5♣ or South passing the double for penalties.

Had North doubled, South would bid 4♡, which makes easily. If East-West push on to 5◇, North doubles for penalties for +500 at least and quite possibly +800 on the ♣K lead.

If you pass 4◇, South is likely to pass, too. You will collect +100 or +150, but that is a paltry amount compared to the +450 available in either major suit game.

Overheard at score-up time: 'Passed in? Passed in??? How did the bidding go?'

22 Curious Curio

There is an unusual feature in the auction on this deal. Can you spot what is unusual about the bidding?

East dealer : Both vulnerable

```
              North
              ♠ J 8 6 4 2
              ♡ 7 6 5 4
              ◇ Q 10 5 4
              ♣ - - -
West                        East
♠ Q 10 9                    ♠ A 7 5 3
♡ K J 9                     ♡ Q 10 8 3 2
◇ K                         ◇ - - -
♣ A Q 9 7 5 3               ♣ J 10 8 2
              South
              ♠ K
              ♡ A
              ◇ A J 9 8 7 6 3 2
              ♣ K 6 4
```

West	North	East	South
		Pass	1◇
Dble	2◇	2♡	3NT
Pass	Pass	4♠	5◇
Pass	Pass	Pass	

The play was straightforward for +620, declarer losing just a spade trick. Both sides can make a slam on this deal. The curious aspect: East-West never mentioned clubs, the only suit in which they can make a slam against best defence.

With the huge disparity in length between the clubs and the majors, West ought to overcall 2♣ rather than double. If a bid of 2◇ or 3◇ or 4◇ comes back to West, a takeout double would then be in order. As a passed hand, East might have chosen 3◇ rather than 2♡. Bidding the enemy suit shows a maximum pass and a choice of contracts. The 3◇ bid by East is justified because of the excellent shape.

There is a useful declarer tip for South when playing in 6◇: *With twelve trumps missing the king, play for the drop.*

Stayman: A convention which allows you to give maximum information to the opponents to assist them in defending against your 3NT contract.

Sorry, partner, I couldn't make it. The aces were in the wrong hand. The opponents had them.

Squeeze without the count: Extra-curricular activity by the countess.

Up-the-line: A way of bidding suits that allows partner to snatch the no-trumps first.

23 North dealer : Both vulnerable

West	North	East	South
	Pass	Pass	Pass
1♡	2♢	3♢ (1)	4♢
Pass	Pass	?	

(1) Maximum pass with heart support

What should East do with:

♠ 9 8 7 4 2
♡ K 10 6 3
♢ K 4
♣ K Q

24 West dealer : Nil vulnerable

West	North	East	South
Pass	Pass	1♠	Dble
2♠	Dble (1)	4♠	?

(1) For takeout, showing both minors

What would you do as South with:

♠ 7
♡ A 8 7 6
♢ A Q J 6
♣ A J 7 6

25 West dealer : North-South vulnerable

West	North	East	South
Pass	Pass	1♡	2NT (1)
4♡	?		

(1) Both minors

What action would you take as North with:

♠ Q 9 8 4 2
♡ 5 4 3
♢ K 5
♣ K Q 8

26 North dealer : East-West vulnerable

West	North	East	South
	1♢	1♡	Pass
2♣	2♢	?	

What would you do as East with:

♠ A Q 6
♡ A J 9 7 3 2
♢ 3
♣ Q 8 4

23 Passing Time

It is uncommon to open in fourth seat only to find that your opponents then reach an unbeatable game, but that is what happened on this deal from the final a national teams championship. Mind you, N-S had to be pushed there.

North dealer : Both vulnerable

```
            North
            ♠ A Q 5
            ♡ 8 5 4
            ◇ Q 9 6 5 3 2
            ♣ 3
West                      East
♠ K 10                    ♠ 9 8 7 4 2
♡ A Q J 7 2               ♡ K 10 6 3
◇ J 8                     ◇ K 4
♣ J 10 9 4                ♣ K Q
            South
            ♠ J 6 3
            ♡ 9
            ◇ A 10 7
            ♣ A 8 7 6 5 2
```

West	North	East	South
	Pass	Pass	Pass
1♡	2◇	3◇ (1)	4◇
Pass	Pass	4♡	Pass
Pass	5◇	Pass	Pass
Dble	Pass	Pass	Pass

(1) Maximum pass, heart support

West won the heart lead and shifted to the ♠K. North, Paul Marston, won and played a club to the ace and ruffed a club. A diamond to the ace was followed by another club ruff. When East's over-ruff was with the king, declarer was home. The spade return was taken by the queen and the ◇Q drew the missing trump. A heart ruff was followed by another club ruff and dummy was high, +750.

East should have passed 4◇. This is a sound principle for competitive bidding: *Do not bid the same values twice.* East's 3◇ had shown the strength and if partner did not want to bid 4♡, so be it.

At the other table, North opened 2◇, weak, raised to 3◇ by South. East-West bought the hand in 3♡, two down for −200 but + 11 Imps.

'Opening bid': The first mistake in the auction.

'Response': The second mistake in the auction.

24 Trouble With Double

This deal arose in a national teams championship during the qualifying rounds:

West dealer : Nil vulnerable

```
          North
          ♠ J 9
          ♡ 10 2
          ◇ K 10 5 4 3
          ♣ K Q 9 8
West                    East
♠ Q 5 3                 ♠ A K 10 8 6 4 2
♡ K J 3                 ♡ Q 9 5 4
◇ 9 8 7 2               ◇ - - -
♣ 10 4 2                ♣ 5 3
          South
          ♠ 7
          ♡ A 8 7 6
          ◇ A Q J 6
          ♣ A J 7 6
```

At one table the bidding went:

West	North	East	South
Pass	Pass	1♠	Dble
2♠	Dble (1)	4♠	Dble
Pass	Pass	Pass	

(1) For takeout, both minors

Declarer had no difficulty in making ten tricks for +590. He lost just two clubs and one heart. Despite having three aces, South's decision to double 4♠ was a poor one. Far better would be 4NT, asking for North's longer minor.

North would bid 5◇, which cannot be defeated.

At several tables it went:

West	North	East	South
Pass	Pass	4♠	Dble (1)
Pass	4NT (2)	Pass	5♣ (3)
Pass	Pass	Dble	All pass

(1) For takeout (modern style)
(2) For takeout, playable in at least two suits
(3) 5◇, stronger suit, is better

A double of 4NT would indicate a strong hand. The pass of 4NT and double of 5♣ should be taken as lead-directing, based usually on a void. West should therefore lead the longest unbid suit. Here that would be diamonds, which would defeat 5♣. At many tables 5♣ doubled was made when West did not find the desired lead. Indeed, at one table South redoubled and made eleven tricks.

Conflicting uses of a double are not grounds for divorce.

If at first you don't succeed, then bridge is a better hobby than sky-diving.

The password is 'No bid'.

25 A sacrificial offering

When should you sacrifice against their game contract? It is worthwhile when your sacrifice might succeed, or when their contract will probably make and the cost of your sacrifice is less than the value of their contract.

This deal from a national pairs event with IMP-scoring featured such a decision:

West dealer : N-S vulnerable

```
              North
              ♠ Q 9 8 4 2
              ♡ 5 4 3
              ◇ K 5
              ♣ K Q 8
West                     East
♠ 7 5                    ♠ K J 6 3
♡ K 10 8 7 6             ♡ A Q J 9 2
◇ A 7 4                  ◇ J 9 6
♣ 10 6 4                 ♣ 7
              South
              ♠ A 10
              ♡ - - -
              ◇ Q 10 8 3 2
              ♣ A J 9 5 3 2
```

West	North	East	South
Pass	Pass	1♡	2NT (1)
4♡	5♣	All pass	

(1) Unusual 2NT, both minors

It is normally unsound to sacrifice with a balanced hand and particularly so with only three-card support for one of partner's suits. What persuaded North to breach these principles and reach the successful game?

The 2NT was at unfavourable vulnerability, always a sign that partner will have sound values. In addition South bid 2NT opposite a passed hand, another strong indication of a useful hand. With three top honours in partner's suits, North judged that 5♣ would not be expensive and might make on a lucky day.

With the diamond layout favourable, declarer lost just one diamond and one spade for +600. That was worth 6 Imps in the open field where the datum was 360 North-South. If East-West sacrifice in 5♡ over 5♣, the penalty should be 300 or 500. The datum in the women's was 70 North-South.

'Unusual 2NT': Any time partner bids 2NT and it happens to be the right bid.

26 Silent Partners

Here is a useful guide when you have no clear-cut action: With a choice of making a uni-directional bid or one that allows several options, choose the latter. Had East heeded this advice, a vulnerable game would have been found on this deal from the final of a national teams championship:

North dealer : E-W vulnerable

```
            North
            ♠ K 7
            ♡ Q 8 5
            ◇ K J 8 6 5 4 2
            ♣ K
West                    East
♠ 10 5 4 2              ♠ A Q 6
♡ - - -                 ♡ A J 9 7 3 2
◇ A Q 9                 ◇ 3
♣ A 9 7 6 5 2           ♣ Q 8 4
            South
            ♠ J 9 8 3
            ♡ K 10 6 4
            ◇ 10 7
            ♣ J 10 3
```

West	North	East	South
	1◇	1♡	Pass
2♣	2◇	3♡	All pass

Once West bid 2♣ and East had significant club support, East's hand has become quite powerful. How to describe that to partner? If the jump to 3♡

was intended to imply six hearts and a club fit, West did not get the message and became a silent partner.

East might have raised to 3♣ to show the club fit. A better move for East would be 3◇ over 2◇. That shows a strong hand and gives West a number of choices. On the actual hand, West would have rebid 3NT, which is unbeatable. 3♡ was one down, –100.

At the other table:

West	North	East	South
	1◇	1♡	1♠
Pass?	2◇	2♡	Pass
Pass?	3◇	All pass	

Cowed by the vulnerability and the void in partner's suit, West became another silent partner. No one can promise West safety by bidding here, but passing does not guarantee success either. When East raised another bid opposite a possibly worthless hand, West could still not muster a bid. 3◇ was three down, –150.

'To bid or not to bid? That is the question.'
'And the answer is, Bid!'.

27   North dealer : East-West vulnerable

West	North	East	South
	4♡	?	

What should East do with:

♠ A Q J 9 8
♡ - - -
♢ J 10 8 6 5 3 2
♣ 4

28   South dealer : East-West vulnerable

West	North	East	South
			4♡
Pass	Pass	4♠	Pass
?			

What would you do as West with:

♠ 5
♡ K 6 3
♢ A 8 7 4 2
♣ A K 8 7

29   West dealer : Both vulnerable

West	North	East	South
Pass	Pass	3♦	?

What action would you take as South with:

♠ A Q 5 2
♡ K 3
♦ Q
♣ K Q J 10 9 8

30   South dealer : East-West vulnerable

West	North	East	South
			1♣
Pass	5♣	?	

What would you do as East with:

♠ A 6 5 4 3
♡ K J 9 8 7
♦ Q
♣ A 10

27 The Call of the Wild

This was a wild deal from a national pairs selection event with IMP scoring:

North dealer : E-W vulnerable

```
        North
        ♠ K 5
        ♡ K 10 9 8 7 6 5 2
        ♢ 9
        ♣ K 6
West              East
♠ 10 6 3          ♠ A Q J 9 8
♡ Q J             ♡ - - -
♢ A Q 7 4         ♢ J 10 8 6 5 3 2
♣ A 10 7 3        ♣ 4
        South
        ♠ 7 4 2
        ♡ A 4 3
        ♢ K
        ♣ Q J 9 8 5 2
```

With only 21 HCP, including the useless ♡Q-J, East-West can make 7♠ or 7♢. That is lucky, but 6♠/6♢ is reasonable. North-South have a cheap sacrifice and can make nine tricks in hearts. It is not easy for East-West to find their way after North opens 4♡. This was the most popular sequence in the open section:

West	North	East	South
	4♡	4♠	5♡
5♠	Pass	Pass	Pass

This was worth around +20 Imps (scoring against the field). The best result for East-West:

West	North	East	South
	4♡	4♠	5♡
5♠	6♡	6♠	All pass

Thirteen tricks, +1460 and +98 Imps to East-West. This was the worst result for E-W:

West	North	East	South
	4♡	All pass	

The ♠A was led and so 4♡ made ten tricks for +420 and −102 Imps to East-West.

You might be satisfied with the majority choice of 4♠, but that is not my view. When I gave the problem to my wife, Suzie, she produced a better bid for East than any of the above. "Why not 4NT for takeout?" she said. "If partner bids 5♣, I can remove to 5♢ showing diamonds and spades, presumably at least five spades and at least six diamonds." Being able to show both suits has to be the best chance to find the right spot for E-W.

'Flat board': The opponents made the same blunders as your side.

28 A Fortunate Life

This deal from a national Swiss Teams Championship in 2002 illustrates several issues after an opening pre-empt:

South dealer : E-W vulnerable

```
          North
          ♠ Q J 9 3
          ♡ 10 8
          ◊ K J 10 9
          ♣ J 9 6

West                    East
♠ 5                     ♠ A K 10 6 2
♡ K 6 3                 ♡ 4
◊ A 8 7 4 2             ◊ Q
♣ A K 8 7              ♣ Q 10 5 4 3 2

          South
          ♠ 8 7 4
          ♡ A Q J 9 7 5 2
          ◊ 6 5 3
          ♣ - - -
```

The first question is what should South do? Many opened 3♡ but at the vulnerability, 4♡ is likely to be more damaging. Next, if South opens 3♡, what should West do? The majority opted for pass (double would be for takeout). Viewing the world through rose-tinted glasses, I chose 3NT, which had a fortunate outcome:

West	North	East	South
			3♡
3NT	Pass	4♣	Pass
5♣	Pass	6♣	All pass

This was worth 1370 against 620 at the other table. Datum (average) was E-W 610.

Two top players came to grief after a 4♡ opening:

West	North	East	South
			4♡
Pass	Pass	4♠	Pass
5♠	Pass	Pass	Pass

After 4♡ : Pass : Pass, most top players would choose 4♠ on the East cards. While 4♠ can be made (play ♠A, ♠K and a third spade after coming on lead), 5♠ was one too high.

5♠ was an ill-judged bid. If you are going to bid on – and that is not clear-cut, as East may have stretched to bid 4♠ – a much better move is 5♡. If 6♠ is the right contract, 5♡ will not preclude that. Over 5♡, East has an easy 6♣. Mind you, East was not blameless. Over 5♠, East could certainly justify 6♣.

Asking bid: A bid which asks partner to make the wrong decision instead of you.

29 Preferred Takeout

Neither North-South pair would have been pleased with the outcome on this deal from a 2002 national teams event:

West dealer : Both vulnerable

```
                North
                ♠ K 9 6 3
                ♡ 10 8 7 5 4
                ◇ K J
                ♣ A 5
West                        East
♠ J 10 8                    ♠ 7 4
♡ A J 9 6 2                 ♡ Q
◇ 10 9 3                    ◇ A 8 7 6 5 4 2
♣ 7 6                       ♣ 4 3 2
                South
                ♠ A Q 5 2
                ♡ K 3
                ◇ Q
                ♣ K Q J 10 9 8
```

West	North	East	South
Pass	Pass	3◇	4♣
Pass	5♣	All pass	

West led ◇10. East won ◇A and switched to the ♡Q. South played low but West rose with the ♡A and gave East a heart ruff. One down.

It is tempting to bid 4♣ but a superior action is to double 3◇ for takeout. In reply North should bid 4◇ with both majors.

It follows that if North replies with an unwanted 4♡, South should bid 5♣, as North will not hold spades and hearts.

Doubling 3◇ should lead to 4♠. Had South doubled the auction might go:

West	North	East	South
Pass	Pass	3◇	Dble
Pass	4◇	Pass	4♠
Pass	Pass	Pass	

At the other table 4♠ was reached and the defence started the same way: diamond to the ace, switch to the ♡Q. Declarer covered with the king. That would have been right if East had Q-J doubleton but was not a winner here. If declarer plays low on the ♡Q, 4♠ cannot be defeated.

West took the ♡A, cashed the ♡J and played a third heart. East ruffed with the ♠7 and that promoted a trump trick for West. One down. No swing.

"What do you think is the worst part of my game?"
"The bridge."

Courage: Bidding one more than your cards are worth.
Foolhardiness: Bidding two more than your cards are worth.

30 The Axe-Man Cometh

There is a time to bid and a time to pass. Witness this deal which arose in the semi-finals of a national teams event:

South dealer : E-W vulnerable

```
              North
              ♠ - - -
              ♡ A 10 4
              ◇ 10 7 5
              ♣ Q 9 7 5 4 3 2

West                      East
♠ K 10 9 8                ♠ A 6 5 4 3
♡ 2                       ♡ K J 9 8 7
◇ K 9 8 6 4 3 2           ◇ Q
♣ J                       ♣ A 10

              South
              ♠ Q J 7 2
              ♡ Q 6 5 3
              ◇ A J
              ♣ K 8 6
```

West	North	East	South
			1♣
Pass	5♣	Dble	Pass
5◇	Dble	5♡	Dble
5♠	Dble	All pass	

If East's double is for penalties, then West should pass. However, most modern players use double for takeout after any pre-emptive bid, even at the five-level. That is what prompted West to bid 5◇ on

the 7-card suit, which ultimately led to the disaster in 5♠ doubled for –800.

If double is for takeout, should East double? The doubleton club holding is a drawback and the hand is quite skimpy. As West could not bid over 1♣ it is ambitious to look for a 5-level contract with such values.

The answer is that East should have been perfectly safe in doubling. West's failure to bid over 1♣ indicated either an abjectly weak hand or a hand with no 6+ suit and no decent 5-card suit. East's reasonable expectation is that West would be sure to leave the double in for penalties.

West should have bid something over 1♣ despite the vulnerability. Bid 1◇, bid 2◇ or bid 3◇, but bid something.

My partner played really well today. Regrettably, the game wasn't bridge.

"Congratulations on your win"
"Thanks but we were lucky"
"Really?"
"Yes, partner played well."

31   West dealer : East-West vulnerable

West	North	East	South
2♡	2♠	?	

What should East do with:

♠ J 10 9 7 6
♡ A Q 4
◇ 2
♣ Q 10 5 3

32   South dealer : East-West vulnerable

West	North	East	South
			Pass
Pass	1◇	Dble	1♠
Pass	2◇	3◇	?

What would you do as South with:

♠ Q J 9 8 7
♡ 7
◇ 9 7 6 4 2
♣ Q J

33 North dealer : Both vulnerable

West	North	East	South
	2◇ (1)	Pass	?

(1) Weak two in diamonds

What should South do with:

♠ A Q 10
♡ 9
◇ 10 7 6 3
♣ A J 10 4 3

34 West dealer : Both vulnerable

West	North	East	South
2◇ (1)	3◇	3NT	4♣
Pass	?		

(1) Weak two in diamonds

What would you do as North with:

♠ A K J 10 3 2
♡ A K Q J 4 3
◇ - - -
♣ Q

31 Raising the Ante

This deal is from a Swiss Pairs event with IMP scoring.

West dealer : E-W vulnerable

```
            North
            ♠ A K Q 8 3
            ♡ 5 3
            ◇ K J 5
            ♣ 7 6 4
West                    East
♠ 2                    ♠ J 10 9 7 6
♡ K J 10 9 7 6 2       ♡ A Q 4
◇ 10 6                 ◇ 2
♣ 9 8 2                ♣ Q 10 5 3
            South
            ♠ 5 4
            ♡ 8
            ◇ A Q 9 8 7 4 3
            ♣ A K J
```

West	North	East	South
2♡	2♠	Pass	3◇
Pass	4◇	Pass	4NT (1)
Pass	5♡ (2)	Pass	6◇
Pass	Pass	Pass	

(1) Roman Key Card Blackwood
(2) Two key cards, no ◇Q

N-S were given an easy ride. They had no trouble locating their trump fit and finding the controls needed. There was nothing to the play and South chalked up an easy slam.

At any other vulnerability, West might open 3♡, but here 2♡, a weak two, was eminently reasonable. East was the one to do more by competing with 3♡ over 2♠. At favourable vulnerability a jump to 4♡ would not be excessive. A sound principle for competitive bidding is to bid for nine tricks if your side has nine trumps and bid for ten tricks if your side has ten trumps.

How much harder would the auction have been if East had simply raised the bidding to the three-level. If South bids 4◇, North cannot show diamond support and also the number of key-cards without some very sophisticated understandings. A bid of 4♡ over 4◇ as a strong diamond raise would be helpful. If North simply raises to 5◇, South might take the plunge and bid 6◇, but that could work out badly on other days.

Pass is a four-letter word.

'Overcall': The first mistake by the defending side.

Team-mates: The Gripes of Wrath

32 Be a mouse that roars

When you play teams or rubber bridge, accuracy in the slam department is worth loads of points. Because slams occur rarely, pairs do not have the same experience with slam bidding as for games or part-scores. Pairs should spend more time practising slam bidding.

This deal arose in a national Swiss pairs championship:

South dealer : E-W vulnerable

```
                North
                ♠ K 10 5
                ♡ - - -
                ◇ A K Q J 8 5
                ♣ 9 7 6 5
West                        East
♠ 6 4 3 2                   ♠ A
♡ J 10 5 2                  ♡ A K Q 9 8 6 4 3
◇ 10 3                      ◇ - - -
♣ K 8 3                     ♣ A 10 4 2
                South
                ♠ Q J 9 8 7
                ♡ 7
                ◇ 9 7 6 4 2
                ♣ Q J
```

West	North	East	South
			Pass
Pass	1◇	Dble	1♠
Pass	2◇	3◇	4◇
4♡	Pass	6♡	All pass

East is far too strong to jump straight to 4♡. To show the powerhouse, double first and bid their suit next.

After East's 3◇ showed a game-going hand, South's 4◇ was a mouse-like effort. At the vulnerability South should jump to 5◇ like a lion. That would silence West and it would much tougher now to bid the laydown 6♡, worth 11 Imps with the datum (average) being E-W 930.

Over 4◇, West did well to bid 4♡ and it was not tough for East to bid 6♡. The thought of 7♡ might flit through your mind, but if West had as much as ♡J-10-x-x and ♣K-Q-x or similar, that would be enough to bid 2♡ over 1♠. The failure to bid 2♡ then and the 4♡ bid now limited West to a very modest collection. Upon tabling his hand after the opening lead, East said, 'When I picked these cards up, I did not expect to be dummy in a heart contract.'

What are you, a man or a mouse? Squeak up.

33 Training for the High Jump

These deals from a national Swiss pairs championship illustrate the benefits of the immediate jump to game when holding a good fit with partner.

North dealer : Both vulnerable

```
              North
              ♠ K J 2
              ♡ 10 7
              ◇ K Q 9 5 4 2
              ♣ 9 7
West                     East
♠ 7 5                    ♠ 9 8 6 4 3
♡ A K Q J 4 3 2          ♡ 8 6 5
◇ ---                    ◇ A J 8
♣ K Q 5 2                ♣ 8 6
              South
              ♠ A Q 10
              ♡ 9
              ◇ 10 7 6 3
              ♣ A J 10 4 3
```

West	North	East	South
	2◇ (1)	Pass	5◇!
5♡	Pass	Pass	Dble!
Pass	Pass	Pass	

(1) Weak two in diamonds

Lead: ◇K

With the opponents sure to have a 9+ fit in hearts, South naturally jumped straight to 5◇. Who can blame West for bidding 5♡? Despite the ◇K lead, West could not avoid three losers. N-S +200 and +13 Imps (datum E-W 570).

South dealer : E-W vulnerable

```
              North
              ♠ 10 9
              ♡ K J 9
              ◇ 8 2
              ♣ A Q J 8 7 6
West                     East
♠ A J 5 3                ♠ Q 8 6 4
♡ Q 10 8 6 5 4 2         ♡ A 7 3
◇ 10 5                   ◇ K Q J 4 3
♣ ---                    ♣ K
              South
              ♠ K 7 2
              ♡ ---
              ◇ A 9 7 6
              ♣ 10 9 5 4 3 2
```

West	North	East	South
			Pass
Pass	1♣ (1)	Dble	5♣!
5♡	Pass	Pass	Dble!
Pass	Pass	Pass	

Declarer had to lose two hearts and a diamond. N-S +200 and +4 Imps (datum N-S 60).

The Chance Card in bridge: With a weak hand and a strong trump fit, go directly to game, do not pass game but do collect 200.

'I am thinking of patenting a game that is similar to, but does not really resemble, bridge.'
'No point. My partner plays that already.'

34 Freak Show

This freak deal arose in a Swiss teams event:

West dealer : Both vulnerable

```
          North
          ♠ A K J 10 3 2
          ♡ A K Q J 4 3
          ◇ - - -
          ♣ Q
West                    East
♠ 8 6 4                 ♠ 9
♡ 10 5                  ♡ 8 7 6 2
◇ A Q J 10 8 5          ◇ K 9 7 3 2
♣ 9 5                   ♣ A 4 3
          South
          ♠ Q 7 5
          ♡ 9
          ◇ 6 4
          ♣ K J 10 8 7 6 2
```

West	North	East	South
2◇ (1)	3◇	3NT	4♣
Pass	6◇!	Pass	6♠
Pass	Pass	7◇	Dble
Pass	Pass	Pass	

(1) Weak two in diamonds

Over 2◇, North bid 3◇ to show both majors. After 3NT, South offered clubs as an option before showing the spade support. North's jump to 6◇, asking South to choose between 6♡ and 6♠, is a sensible practical move. There is mild risk involved (South might not have support for either major and might lack the ♠Q), but if you cannot accept risk, this game is not for you. 6♡ or 6♠ is unbeatable for North-South for +1430 and East did well to sacrifice in 7◇, which cost only 1100.

South's double of 7◇ is important. To pass might suggest the ♣A and tempt North to bid seven.

At the other table:

West	North	East	South
3◇	4◇	5♣ (1)	Pass
Pass	6◇	7◇	Pass
Pass	Dble	All pass	

(1) An excellent lead-directing bid by East en route to 5◇

At one table everyone bid only diamonds except for South:

West	North	East	South
3◇	4◇	5◇	Dble
Pass	6◇	Pass	6♠
Pass	Pass	Pass	

Bridge club sign: 'Seven days without bridge makes one weak.'

Pre-emptive jump: An important move in defence when partner tries to kick you.

PART 3: Improve Your Opening Leads

35 West dealer : Nil vulnerable

West	North	East	South
Pass	Pass	1♡	1♠
2◇	2♠	3◇	3♠
Pass	Pass	Pass	

What should West lead from:

♠ Q J 4 2
♡ Q
◇ K Q 10 6 2
♣ J 8 3

36 (a) Pairs : North dealer : Nil vulnerable

West	North	East	South
	Pass	Pass	2♡ (1)
Pass	3♡	Dble	All pass

(1) Weak two

What would you lead as West from:

♠ A Q
♡ K 6 3
◇ Q 10 7 2
♣ Q 10 8 4

36 (b) Pairs: South opens 1♠, showing diamonds and 9-14 points. North relays and finds South has a maximum with a 3-2-6-2 pattern with at least the queen in every suit except clubs. North signs off in 5♠. What would you lead as West from:

♠ 9 8 6
♡ Q 10 9 3
◇ 4
♣ A Q 9 7 2

37   Teams : North dealer : East-West vulnerable

West	North	East	South
	1◇	1♡	2♣
4♡	5♣	5♡	6♣
Pass	Pass	Pass	

What would you lead as West from:

♠ 9 8 4
♡ A K J 7 6 5 3
◇ J 5
♣ J

38   Pairs : East dealer : Nil vulnerable

West	North	East	South
		1♣	1♠
2♡	2♠	3♡	3♠
4♡	4♠	Dble	All pass

What should West lead from:

♠ 6
♡ Q J 8 6 4 2
◇ K 5
♣ J 7 6 3

35 Shipper comes in

Occasionally I am favoured with a game on OKbridge with Bill Haughie (pronounced 'Hoy', so his nickname is 'Shipper'). A misguided lead gave him an easy run on this deal:

West dealer : Nil vulnerable

```
              North
              ♠ K 5 3
              ♡ J 9 7
              ◇ J 7 4 3
              ♣ A 6 5
West                        East
♠ Q J 4 2                   ♠ 9
♡ Q                         ♡ A 8 6 5 4
◇ K Q 10 6 2                ◇ A 9 8 5
♣ J 8 3                     ♣ Q 9 2
              South
              Haughie
              ♠ A 10 8 7 6
              ♡ K 10 3 2
              ◇ - - -
              ♣ K 10 7 4
```

West	North	East	South
Pass	Pass	1♡	1♠
2◇	2♠	3◇	3♠
Pass	Pass	Pass	

West led the ♡Q to East's ace and ruffed the heart return. West shifted to ◇K at trick 3, ruffed by Haughie, who played the ♠K, ♠A, ♡K and ♡10, discarding a club from dummy.

Then came a club to the ace, club to the king and a club ruff. He finished with ten tricks for +170 and +2.4 Imps.

Burn this into your bridge memory: *Trump length, lead length*. West figured to make two trump tricks by power. The heart ruff did not add to West's trick tally.

Suppose West leads the ◇K, ruffed by South. Declarer might cross to dummy with a club to the ace to run the ♡9 for a finesse. That would allow the defence to prevail. When the ♡9 loses to the queen and another diamond is led, the defence is in control and 3♠ can be defeated.

Opening lead: First mistake in the play of the cards.

What do you need to tell partner who has two black eyes?
Answer: Nothing. You've told him twice already.

Witticism: A flash in the pen.
Prison streaker: The same.

Partner: The ultimate euphemism.

36 Leading Question

Ishmael Del'Monte and Paul Marston won the Pacific-Asian Pairs in 2002. These deals are from the Final.

North dealer : Nil vulnerable

```
            North
            ♠ J 10 5 4 3
            ♡ J 10 7
            ◇ K 5 4
            ♣ A J
West                      East
♠ A Q                     ♠ 9 8 7 6
♡ K 6 3                   ♡ Q
◇ Q 10 7 2                ◇ A 9 3
♣ Q 10 8 4                ♣ K 9 7 3 2
            South
            ♠ K 2
            ♡ A 9 8 5 4 2
            ◇ J 8 6
            ♣ 6 5
```

West	North	East	South
	Pass	Pass	2♡ (1)
Pass	3♡	Dble	All pass

(1) Weak two

A trump or a minor suit lead can yield six tricks for +300. The ♣4, stronger suit, is a sensible choice. West chose the fatal lead of the ♠A. South won the ♠Q continuation and made ten tricks, +630.

Relay systems can pinpoint shape, but there is a price to pay.

Giving too much information produced a below-average board for Del'Monte – Marston:

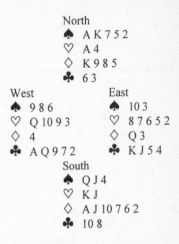

```
            North
            ♠ A K 7 5 2
            ♡ A 4
            ◇ K 9 8 5
            ♣ 6 3
West                      East
♠ 9 8 6                   ♠ 10 3
♡ Q 10 9 3                ♡ 8 7 6 5 2
◇ 4                       ◇ Q 3
♣ A Q 9 7 2               ♣ K J 5 4
            South
            ♠ Q J 4
            ♡ K J
            ◇ A J 10 7 6 2
            ♣ 10 8
```

Marston, South, opened 1♠, showing diamonds and 9-14 points. Del'Monte relayed and found South with a 3-2-6-2 maximum and at least the queen in every suit except clubs. Armed with this information West knew that the ♣K had to be with North or with East. Accordingly he had no trouble leading ♣A and another club. This held 5♠ to eleven tricks while declarer will make all thirteen tricks without a club lead.

37 The Phantom Menace

This was an exciting deal from the final of a national teams championship:

North dealer : E-W vulnerable

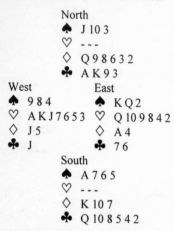

```
                North
                ♠ J 10 3
                ♡ - - -
                ◇ Q 9 8 6 3 2
                ♣ A K 9 3
West                        East
♠ 9 8 4                     ♠ K Q 2
♡ A K J 7 6 5 3             ♡ Q 10 9 8 4 2
◇ J 5                       ◇ A 4
♣ J                         ♣ 7 6
                South
                ♠ A 7 6 5
                ♡ - - -
                ◇ K 10 7
                ♣ Q 10 8 5 4 2
```

At one table South scored +420 in 5♣ after 1◇ : 1♡ : 2♣ : 4♡, 5♣ : All pass. The other table:

West	North	East	South
	1◇	1♡	2♣
4♡	5♣	5♡	6♣
6♡	Pass	Pass	Dble
Pass	Pass	Pass	

Although the defence can take this three down for +800, it is not so surprising that declarer lost just one trick in spades. Still, that was +500 to North-South and a gain of 2 Imps.

Opposite a pre-emptive raise to 4♡, East cannot expect to make 5♡ and should pass 5♣.

As for West it is wrong for the weak hand to take the decision ahead of partner. West should realise that, with no more than the queen in hearts, East will have significant values elsewhere for an overcall at unfavourable vulnerability. It was highly likely that 6♡ would be a phantom sacrifice.

West should pass 6♣ and East will pass, too. A double would call for a diamond lead and East is not anxious for that.

Although the problem did not arise, West has an easy spade lead against 6♣. At least one of the opponents will be void in hearts, if not both. As dummy bid diamonds and the singleton ♣J does not appeal, that leaves a spade lead. That would be enough to put paid to 6♣. So 6♡ was −500 instead of +50 and +10 Imps by defending 6♣.

There is not much difference between the chance of winning the lottery and the chance of partner finding the right lead.

38 The Rule of Suit Length Parity

The first question is, 'What sort of hand will opener have for this sequence?' Not 15+ points and a balanced hand. With that, opener would bid 4♡ (partner does not know that your 2♡ bid is a little light). That leaves a minimum opening, club length and possibly no more than 3-card heart support.

The next question is what to lead. As your side has nine hearts and probably nine clubs, that gives you at least 18 cards in hearts and clubs. Therefore the opponents must have 18 cards in spades and diamonds.

The rule of suit length parity: *Whatever length you and partner have in your two longest combined suits, the opponents have the same total length in their two longest combined suits.*

This sounds pretty impressive but is quite obvious. If in your 26 combined cards, you and partner have 18 cards in hearts-clubs, you have only 8 cards between you in spades-diamonds. The opponents must therefore have 18 cards in spades-diamonds. This principle is important: If you have a double fit, so do the opponents.

That means a trump lead is out and so is the ♢K. Partner cannot have length in clubs, support for hearts, enough spades to double them and also ♢A-x-x to give you a ruff. Of your side's suits, the obvious choice is a heart. Lead the ♡Q in case dummy has ♡K-10.

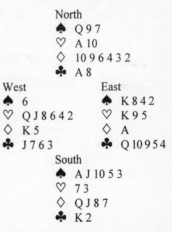

```
              North
              ♠ Q 9 7
              ♡ A 10
              ♢ 10 9 6 4 3 2
              ♣ A 8
West                      East
♠ 6                       ♠ K 8 4 2
♡ Q J 8 6 4 2             ♡ K 9 5
♢ K 5                     ♢ A
♣ J 7 6 3                 ♣ Q 10 9 5 4
              South
              ♠ A J 10 5 3
              ♡ 7 3
              ♢ Q J 8 7
              ♣ K 2
```

As it happens, a heart lead is necessary to beat the contract. At the table the ♢K lead was not a star-studded success and declarer wrapped up 12 tricks.

Unlucky choice: Synonym for partner's lead.

39   East dealer : Both vulnerable

West	North	East	South
		Pass	Pass
Pass	1♦	Pass	1♡
Pass	2♡	Pass	2NT (1)
Pass	3♦ (2)	Pass	4♡
Pass	Pass	Pass	

(1) Asking about trump length
(2) 3 hearts and 5+ diamonds

What should West lead from:

♠ K J 8 5
♡ K 9 4
♦ 10 6 5
♣ 9 7 3

40   West dealer : North-South vulnerable

West	North	East	South
Pass	Pass	1♠	2♡
Pass	2♠ (1)	Pass	4♡
Pass	Pass	Pass	

(1) Good raise to 3♡

What would you lead as West from:

♠ 6 2
♡ J 9
♦ 10 8 7 6
♣ Q J 9 6 2

41   West dealer : Nil vulnerable

West	North	East	South
Pass	Pass	Pass	2♦ (1)
Pass	2♡ (2)	Pass	2♠
Pass	3♦	Pass	3♡
Pass	3♠	Pass	4♣ (3)
Pass	4♡ (3)	Pass	6♠
Pass	Pass	Pass	

(1) Artificial, very strong
(2) Artificial, weak hand
(3) Cue-bid, first-round control

What would you lead as West from:
♠ 8 6 4
♡ Q 5 2
♦ A K 9 2
♣ 9 6 2

42   East dealer : Both vulnerable

West	North	East	South
		Pass	1♣
Pass	1♠	Pass	2♦
Pass	3♦ (1)	Pass	3NT
Pass	4♣	Pass	6♣
Pass	Pass	Dble	Rdble
Pass	Pass	Pass	

(1) Forcing to game

What would you lead as West from:
♠ Q 5 2
♡ Q 8 7 5
♦ 10 7 6 5 4
♣ 6

39 Take Me To Your Leader

The opening lead was critical on this deal from the final of a national teams championship:

East dealer : Both vulnerable

```
              North
              ♠ 6 2
              ♡ A 8 7
              ◇ A K Q 7 2
              ♣ J 6 5
West                      East
♠ K J 8 5                 ♠ 10 9 7 4 3
♡ K 9 4                   ♡ Q 6
◇ 10 6 5                  ◇ J 9
♣ 9 7 3                   ♣ A K 8 2
              South
              ♠ A Q
              ♡ J 10 5 3 2
              ◇ 8 4 3
              ♣ Q 10 4
```

West	North	East	South
		Pass	Pass
Pass	1◇	Pass	1♡
Pass	2♡	Pass	2NT (1)
Pass	3◇ (2)	Pass	4♡
Pass	Pass	Pass	

(1) Asking about trump length
(2) 3 hearts and 5+ diamonds

West led the ♡4, ducked to the queen. East cashed the ♣K, ♣A and played a third club. South won this and led the ♡J: ♡K, ♡A. The last trump was drawn and the diamonds enabled South to discard the ♠Q for +620.

When dummy has shown a long suit and you cannot stop the run of that suit, it is usually best to lead one of the unbid suits. Do not lead a trump and do not lead dummy's long suit. As North has long diamonds, West should choose a black suit lead. Club to the king and a spade switch will beat 4♡, as will three rounds of clubs and another club when in with the ♡Q. South can succeed on a spade lead by playing East for honour doubleton. Not so easy.

At the other table:

West	North	East	South
		Pass	Pass
Pass	1NT	Pass	2◇ (1)
Pass	2♡	Pass	2NT (2)
Pass	4♡	All pass	

(1) Transfer to hearts
(2) Inviting game with 5 hearts

East led the ♣A and switched to a spade, queen, king. The contract now went two down for +200 and +13 Imps.

'Lead-out-of-turn': attempt to prevent partner from making the first mistake.

40 The dog that didn't bark

If partner opens in third seat and the opponents bid game, chances are that partner has opened light. As partner should have a strong suit to justify opening light, it makes sense to lead partner's suit, but perhaps there are clues to suggest that some other lead could be right.

On this deal from a national selection event every N-S pair reached 4♡. All but one made it.

West dealer : N-S vulnerable

```
              North
              ♠ 10 3
              ♡ 10 7 5 4
              ◇ A Q 5 2
              ♣ K 8 7
West                      East
♠ 6 2                     ♠ K Q 8 7 5
♡ J 9                     ♡ 3 2
◇ 10 8 7 6                ◇ K J 9
♣ Q J 9 6 2               ♣ A 5 3
              South
              ♠ A J 9 4
              ♡ A K Q 8 6
              ◇ 4 3
              ♣ 10 4
```

At every table the bidding began:

West	North	East	South
Pass	Pass	1♠	2♡
Pass	?		

One North jumped to 4♡, two bid 3♡, raised to four by South, and two bid 2♠ (strong raise to 3♡) and South jumped to 4♡. At every table but one the opening lead was the ♠6. Declarer captured East's queen, drew trumps in two rounds and led a spade to the ten and king. There were now two discards available to throw two clubs from dummy and so declarer lost just one club, one diamond and one spade, +620.

At the remaining table, where North had bid 2♠ to show the strong heart raise, the opening lead was the ♣Q. The defence collected two club tricks, one spade and the ◇K for one down.

What persuaded West to lead the ♣Q here rather than a spade? If East had wanted a spade lead and nothing else, East would have doubled the artificial 2♠. As East did not double 2♠, East was happy to receive some other lead. That was enough of a clue for West to choose the ♣Q.

Maximum chance of partner finding the best lead: 1-in-13.

41 The expensive diamond

Before making an 'automatic' lead, re-study the auction to see what clues lie there. Many Imps swung on the choice of lead on this deal from the final of a national teams event:

West dealer : Nil vulnerable

```
              North
              ♠ J 2
              ♡ A
              ◇ J 8 7 6 5 4
              ♣ 10 8 5 3
West                        East
♠ 8 6 4                     ♠ 9 7
♡ Q 5 2                     ♡ J 8 7 4
◇ A K 9 2                   ◇ Q 10 3
♣ 9 6 2                     ♣ K Q 7 4
              South
              ♠ A K Q 10 5 3
              ♡ K 10 9 6 3
              ◇ - - -
              ♣ A J
```

West	North	East	South
Pass	Pass	Pass	2◇ (1)
Pass	2♡ (2)	Pass	2♠
Pass	3◇	Pass	3♡
Pass	3♠	Pass	4♣ (3)
Pass	4♡ (3)	Pass	6♠
Pass	Pass	Pass	

(1) Artificial, very strong
(2) Artificial, weak hand
(3) Cue-bid, first-round control
Lead: ◇A

Declarer ruffed the lead, played ♡A, club to the ace and ruffed a low heart in dummy. A low diamond, ruffed, was followed by another low heart, ruffed. After another diamond ruff, declarer drew trumps and claimed the slam, losing just one club. That was worth +980.

The ◇A lead is instinctive but one can find the killing trump lead. North did not raise spades at once, indicating just doubleton support. A trump lead may prevent the ♡Q being ruffed out. There is no rush to cash a diamond. Where can South discard a diamond loser? South's choice of the 4♣ cue-bid suggests a void somewhere, probably in diamonds. With a 6-5-1-1, South would be likely to ask for aces over 3♠.

At the other table the bidding went 1♠ : 1NT, 4♡ : 4♠, Pass for +480. Thus the ◇A lead against 6♠ cost 11 Imps while a trump lead would gain 11.

Opening lead rule-of-thumb: Lead the card nearest your thumb.

42 The Slim-Slam Man

There were hard luck stories a'plenty on this deal from a national Swiss teams event:

East dealer : Both vulnerable

```
            North
            ♠ A 8 7 3
            ♡ J 6
            ◇ A J 9 2
            ♣ K 8 2

West                      East
♠ Q 5 2                   ♠ K J 10 9 6 4
♡ Q 8 7 5                 ♡ K 9 4 2
◇ 10 7 6 5 4              ◇ - - -
♣ 6                       ♣ 7 5 4

            South
            ♠ - - -
            ♡ A 10 3
            ◇ K Q 8 3
            ♣ A Q J 10 9 3
```

7◇, the spot you want to reach, is a superb contract, only to founder on the 5-0 split. At many tables, N-S bid to 6♣ and East doubled, asking for an unusual lead and hoping to score a diamond ruff. South often redoubled and – 400 was a flat board in some matches.

For the auction in the problem, South was about to bid 7◇ over 6♣ when East doubled 6♣. As diamonds had been bid and raised, West should have found the diamond lead but in practice led a club for –1830.

The biggest swing in a match arose when East, made 2♠ doubled for +870 and South made 6♣ doubled at the other table for +1540 and +20 Imps. The remarkable feature is that South received a diamond lead, ruffed by East who switched to a heart. With hopes for slam slim, seemingly non-existent, how did South make 12 tricks?

Young Australian star, Kieran Dyke, was prepared to go two down for a minute chance at success via some nifty flim-flam. After taking the ♡A, he drew trumps, cashed the diamonds and ran his trumps, leaving the ♠A isolated in dummy. His last two cards were the ♡10-3 and dummy had ♠A-8. When both opponents discarded their hearts to hold on to two spades each, Dyke scored the last two tricks with his hearts.

'Fourth best': The lead selected by partner, in contrast to the best lead, the second best lead or the third best lead.

PART 4: Improve Your Defensive Play

43 North dealer : Nil vulnerable

>   North
>   ♠ K Q J
>   ♡ Q 7 3
>   ◇ Q 5 4 3
>   ♣ J 9 8

>   East
>   ♠ 7
>   ♡ 6 5 2
>   ◇ A 9
>   ♣ K Q 10 7 6 5 3

West	North	East	South
	1◇	3♣ (1)	3♡
3♠	4♡	All pass	

(1) Weak jump-overcall

West leads the ♣A. What should East play?

44 North dealer : Nil vulnerable

>   North
>   ♠ K 7 3 2
>   ♡ K Q 10 7 6 5
>   ◇ K J
>   ♣ 10

>   East
>   ♠ 10 5
>   ♡ A J 8 4
>   ◇ A 5 4
>   ♣ K 9 6 3

West	North	East	South
	1♡	Pass	1♠
2♣	3♠	5♣	5♠
Pass	Pass	Dble	All pass

West leads the ◇7: jack – ace. You shift to ♣3: ruffed with the
♠6 – ♣2 – ♣10. South plays the ♠J. West wins with the ♠A
and switches to the ♡9: king – ace. What do you play next?

45 West dealer : East-West vulnerable

       North
       ♠ K J 7 3
       ♡ 5
       ♢ 10 8 6 2
       ♣ 9 6 4 2

West
♠ 9
♡ A K J 10 9 6 4 2
♢ A 9 7 3
♣ - - -

West	North	East	South
1♡	Pass	1NT	2♠
4♡	4♠	Dble	All pass

You, West, lead the ♡A: 5 – 3 – 7. What do you play at trick 2?

46 South dealer : Both vulnerable

       North
       ♠ Q 8 6
       ♡ Q 8 7 5 3
       ♢ A Q J 8
       ♣ 10

West
♠ K 10 4
♡ 4
♢ 10 9 4
♣ A Q 9 8 5 3

West	North	East	South
			1♡
2♣	4♣ (1)	5♣	5♡
Pass	Pass	Pass	

(1) Heart support, strong hand, short in clubs

You, West, lead the ♣A: 10 – king from East – jack. What do you play at trick 2?

43 Signal success suppressed

On the following deal, the defence missed two chances.

North dealer : Nil vulnerable

```
              North
              ♠ K Q J
              ♡ Q 7 3
              ◇ Q 5 4 3
              ♣ J 9 8
West                        East
♠ A 9 5 4 3 2               ♠ 7
♡ J 8                       ♡ 6 5 2
◇ 8 7 6                     ◇ A 9
♣ A 2                       ♣ K Q 10 7 6 5 3
              South
              ♠ 10 8 6
              ♡ A K 10 9 4
              ◇ K J 10 2
              ♣ 4
```

West	North	East	South
	1◇	3♣ (1)	3♡
3♠	4♡	All pass	

(1) Weak jump-overcall

Lead: ♣A

When West played a second club, South ruffed, drew trumps and knocked out the other two aces. As the cards lay, there was no problem after trick 2. +420 was worth 7 Imps (3♡ +140 at the other table).

As East could have raised to 4♠ with doubleton support, there is a case for leading ♠A and ♠2 next (suit preference for clubs). East ruffs, plays a club to the ace and receives another spade ruff. Two down.

After the ♣A lead, there is little point in encouraging clubs. If West has a second club, declarer will ruff. East should give a suit-preference signal, preferably with the ♣Q, an impossible natural card.

If West reads that as asking for spades, ♠A and another spade will beat the contract. If West shifts to a diamond (the *eight* is best, to deny interest in diamonds), East wins and switches to spades to receive the killing ruff. With K-x-x or K-x-x-x in diamonds, leading the lowest diamond would suggest a diamond return.

'Signal': a card played by a defender in the vain hope that partner is watching.

Bridge cynic: One who believes that the world of the bridge administration never changes, only short changes.

If bridge were a foolproof game, what would our partners play?

44 Aid from the enemy

On this deal from the qualifying rounds of a national teams championship, a top class player did not find the winning defence:

North dealer : Nil vulnerable

```
              North
              ♠ K 7 3 2
              ♡ K Q 10 7 6 5
              ◇ K J
              ♣ 10
West                    East
♠ A 4                   ♠ 10 5
♡ 9 3                   ♡ A J 8 4
◇ 7                     ◇ A 5 4
♣ A Q J 8 7 5 4 2       ♣ K 9 6 3
              South
              ♠ Q J 9 8 6
              ♡ 2
              ◇ Q 10 9 8 6 3 2
              ♣ - - -
```

West	North	East	South
	1♡	Pass	1♠
2♣	3♠	5♣	5♠
Pass	Pass	Dble	All pass

Lead: ◇7

West led the ◇7: jack – ace. Back came the ♣3, ruffed by South, West following with ♣2. When South played the ♠J, West won with the ace and switched to the ♡9, ♡K, ♡A. East now had to decide which red suit to return.

South is known to have at most six spades and two hearts. Ignore South being 6-2-5-0 as West then has no more trumps. If South is 5-2-6-0 a heart return is needed while if South is 5-1-7-0, you must bring back a diamond.

There are two clues. The first is in the lead. Why would West lead a doubleton diamond if holding ♠A-x and a singleton heart? The natural lead then would have been a heart.

An even bigger clue is the ♣2 at trick 2, a clear suit preference signal for the lower suit, diamonds. In practice East returned a heart and the contract was one down, +100, a loss of 5 Imps as East-West scored +300 at the other table.

'Suit-preference signal':
A clever card understood by three players at the table. None of these is your partner.

'Gambling 3NT':
Any time partner ends up as declarer in 3NT.

'Deceptive card': Refers to any of the thirteen cards played by partner.

45 The long and the short of it

There was scope for neat defence on this deal from a club duplicate:

West dealer : E-W vulnerable

```
            North
            ♠ K J 7 3
            ♡ 5
            ◇ 10 8 6 2
            ♣ 9 6 4 2
West                     East
♠ 9                      ♠ Q 10 8
♡ A K J 109642           ♡ 3
◇ A 9 7 3                ◇ J 5 4
♣ - - -                  ♣ K J 10 8 7 5
            South
            ♠ A 6 5 4 2
            ♡ Q 8 7
            ◇ K Q
            ♣ A Q 3
```

West	North	East	South
1♡	Pass	1NT	2♠
4♡	4♠	Dble	All pass

Lead: ♡A

West has done well by not bidding on to 5♡ (expectation is two down doubled for −500) and by not leading a low heart at trick 1 in the hope that East might win and return a club. East plays the ♡3 on the ♡A and South the ♡7. How should West continue?

West should continue with a low heart at trick 2. On the bidding partner will not have three hearts. Partner may have a singleton heart and might be able to over-ruff dummy. If the hearts happen to be 2-2 and declarer has the queen, one discard from dummy is hardly likely to help declarer.

If declarer ruffs the heart with the ♠K, East has two trump tricks. If declarer discards from dummy or ruffs low, East scores a cheap trump trick. The ♣J switch will now give West a ruff and now another heart, preferably the ♡K, will promote a trump winner for East.

'Bad break': When partner ends up playing the hand.

Bridge errors are like headlights. The other guy's only seem more glaring than your own.

Howell Movement: A movement for duplicate pairs devised by Fred Bowell shortly before he changed his surname.

'I've had a wonderful game of bridge, thank you, but today wasn't it.'

46 Whom can you trust?

When partner plays an abnormally high card, you must try to deduce the message that partner is trying to give you. Neither East-West pair shone on this deal from the semi-finals of a national teams event:

South dealer : Both vulnerable

```
              North
              ♠ Q 8 6
              ♡ Q 8 7 5 3
              ◇ A Q J 8
              ♣ 10
West                      East
♠ K 10 4                  ♠ A J 9 7
♡ 4                       ♡ - - -
◇ 10 9 4                  ◇ 7 6 5 3
♣ A Q 9 8 5 3             ♣ K 7 6 4 2
              South
              ♠ 5 3 2
              ♡ A K J 10 9 6 2
              ◇ K 2
              ♣ J
```

West	North	East	South
			1♡
2♣	4♣ (1)	5♣	5♡
Pass	Pass	Pass	

(1) Heart support, strong hand, short in clubs

Both Wests started with the ♣A. At one table, East gave a delicate signal with the ♣7 but West switched to the ◇10.

Declarer won in hand, drew trumps and discarded two spade losers on the diamonds. Making 5♡.

At the other table East did much better by playing the ♣K under the ♣A. In the unlikely event that South had ♣Q-x, one discard from dummy was not likely to be useful. This dramatic card should have been read as a clear-cut suit-preference signal, but alas, here too West shifted to a 'safe' ◇10.

Taking the ♣K as a request for a spade switch (high card asks for the high suit), West should switch to the ♠K. That can give the defence three spade tricks and 5♡ is two down.

A low spade would also work. If East inserts the ♠J when declarer plays low from dummy the contract goes two down. If East rises with the ♠A and returns a spade the contract is still one off. Given that the ♣K asks for a spade, the ♠K from West is the best move.

One bridge player + an ounce of courage = a ton of success.

47   South dealer : Nil vulnerable

North
- ♠ 10 5 3
- ♡ J 10
- ♢ K Q J 5 2
- ♣ K 7 4

East
- ♠ J 2
- ♡ Q 7 4
- ♢ 10 9 6 4
- ♣ 9 8 6 2

West	North	East	South
			1♡
2♠*	4♢	Pass	4♡
Pass	Pass	Pass	

*Intermediate, 11-14 points

West leads the ♠K and ♠A, South playing low. West continues with the ♢A and then a low spade. What should East play on that?

48   Pairs : West dealer : Both vulnerable

North
- ♠ A 7 3
- ♡ 5
- ♢ Q 8 4
- ♣ A J 9 7 6 2

West
- ♠ K 10 8 4
- ♡ A 9 7 2
- ♢ 7 6 2
- ♣ 5 4

West	North	East	South
Pass	Pass	1NT*	Pass
Pass	2♣	Pass	2♢
Dble	Pass	Pass	Pass

*15-17 points

You, West, lead the ♢7: 4 – 10 – J. South plays ♣10: 5 – 2 – Q. Partner cashes the ♢A, ♢K and shifts to the ♡3, ♡8 from South and you win with the ♡9. What would you play next?

49   Pairs : North dealer : East-West vulnerable

        North
        ♠ Q J 9 8
        ♡ J 8 4
        ◇ A 7
        ♣ K Q J 6

               East
               ♠ A K 10 4 2
               ♡ A Q 9
               ◇ Q 6
               ♣ 8 5 4

West	North	East	South
	1NT	Dble	2◇
Pass	Pass	2♠	3◇
Pass	Pass	Pass	

West leads the ♠5 and East captures the ♣Q with the ♠K. What do you play next?

50   Pairs : South dealer : Both vulnerable

        North
        ♠ K Q 10 3
        ♡ 9 8 7 6 4
        ◇ - - -
        ♣ 10 9 6 2

West
♠ 9 6 4
♡ A Q 2
◇ 9 8 5 2
♣ A 8 5

West	North	East	South
			1◇
Pass	1♡	Pass	1NT (1)
Pass	Pass	Pass	

(1) 12-14

West leads the ♠6: 10 – J – A. Declarer plays the ♠5: 9 – K – 8, followed by ♣10: J – K – A. How would you continue as West?

47 This defence is a knockout

This deal features a simple defensive manoeuvre:

South dealer : Both vulnerable

```
              North
              ♠ J 10 7 4
              ♡ K Q
              ◇ K Q 8 3
              ♣ J 5 2
West                        East
♠ 9 3                       ♠ Q 8 6
♡ J 9 7 4                   ♡ 10 5 2
◇ 10 9 6 4 2                ◇ 7 5
♣ 9 3                       ♣ A K Q 10 4
              South
              ♠ A K 5 2
              ♡ A 8 6 3
              ◇ A J
              ♣ 8 7 6
```

West	North	East	South
			1NT
Pass	2♣ (1)	Dble (2)	2♡
Pass	3♣ (3)	Pass	3♠
Pass	4♠	All pass	

(1) Asking for a major
(2) Shows strong clubs
(3) Denies a club stopper

Lead: ♣9

East takes the ♣Q, ♣K, ♣A. It is clear to East from South's opening (15-18 points), the points in dummy and the points in the East hand that West cannot have a useful high card and so East plays a fourth club.

When West ruffs with the ♠9 ('uppercut'), it knocks out one of dummy's honours. Now East covers whatever trump is led from dummy and scores a trump trick to defeat 4♠.

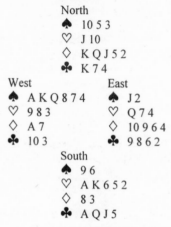

```
              North
              ♠ 10 5 3
              ♡ J 10
              ◇ K Q J 5 2
              ♣ K 7 4
West                        East
♠ A K Q 8 7 4               ♠ J 2
♡ 9 8 3                     ♡ Q 7 4
◇ A 7                       ◇ 10 9 6 4
♣ 10 3                      ♣ 9 8 6 2
              South
              ♠ 9 6
              ♡ A K 6 5 2
              ◇ 8 3
              ♣ A Q J 5
```

South is in 4♡ after West showed a good spade overcall. After cashing two spades and the ◇A West plays a third spade. To beat 4♡ East has to ruff with the ♡7 ('uppercut'). South has to over-ruff with an honour. When East later covers either of dummy's trumps West must come to a trump trick. The deal was supplied by the legendary Tim Seres from a rubber bridge game.

48 The king is dead. Long live the defence.

West dealer : Both vulnerable

```
              North
              ♠ A 7 3
              ♡ 5
              ◇ Q 8 4
              ♣ A J 9 7 6 2
West                      East
♠ K 10 8 4                ♠ 6 5 2
♡ A 9 7 2                 ♡ Q J 6 3
◇ 7 6 2                   ◇ A K 10
♣ 5 4                     ♣ K Q 8
              South
              ♠ Q J 9
              ♡ K 10 8 4
              ◇ J 9 5 3
              ♣ 10 3
```

West	North	East	South
Pass	Pass	1NT	Pass
Pass	2♣	Pass	2◇
Dble	Pass	Pass	Pass

2♣ was explained as 'clubs and another suit', hence South's removal to 2◇. North had simply misbid.

When dummy has a long strong suit that will soon be established and there is only one outside entry to dummy, a common manoeuvre is to attack that entry. After ◇7 ducked to South, ♣10 run to the ♣Q, ◇A, ◇K and ♡3: eight – nine, you can foresee that declarer might play a club to the ace and ruff out East's ♣K, return to dummy via the ♠A and discard losers on the clubs. To prevent this you must attack the ♠A.

A low spade switch will work if partner has the ♠Q but declarer probably has this card. You can place partner with ◇A-K, ♣K-Q and enough in hearts for the 1NT opening. You should therefore switch to the ♠K. If this is taken, the clubs are nullified. If declarer ducks the ♠K, cash the ♡A for +200 and an excellent score.

To sacrifice a high card to knock out a vital entry, is known as the Merrimac Coup. Declarer could have succeeded by playing ♡10 rather than ♡8 and East could have ensured defeat by switching to the ♡Q.

A spade shift by East after ◇A, ◇K will not work. South plays the ♠Q, covered by ♠K and ducked in dummy. Now the ♠A is a firm entry later and the defence can take only 1 spade, 1 heart, 2 diamonds and a club.

Takeout double: what you can do at a casino if you put in quadruple.

49 Surround or surrender

This deal comes from the final of a national pairs event:

North dealer : E-W vulnerable

```
              North
              ♠ Q J 9 8
              ♡ J 8 4
              ◇ A 7
              ♣ K Q J 6
West                    East
♠ 6 5 3                 ♠ A K 10 4 2
♡ 10 7 6 5              ♡ A Q 9
◇ J 3 2                 ◇ Q 6
♣ A 10 2               ♣ 8 5 4
              South
              ♠ 7
              ♡ K 3 2
              ◇ K 10 9 8 5 4
              ♣ 9 7 3
```

West	North	East	South
	1NT	Dble	2◇
Pass	Pass	2♠	3◇
Pass	Pass	Pass	

Lead: ♠5

East found the only defence to defeat 3◇. He won trick 1 with the ♠K and switched to the ♡Q. With no other suit at all attractive, it is right to shift to a heart, but it is not instinctive to start with the queen. East was playing for partner to hold the ♡K or an entry plus the ♡10.

Declarer's king won the trick. A diamond to the ace and a diamond to the king followed. When declarer played a club, West took the ace and returned a heart. The defence thus scored one spade, two hearts, a diamond and a club.

Note that the ♡Q is the only card which will suffice. If you play ♡A and a low heart, declarer ducks and makes two heart tricks. The same happens if you shift to the ♡9. Declarer can duck in hand, win with the jack and still has ♡K-3 to protect the suit.

The ♡Q is a 'surrounding' play. When dummy holds the 9 or higher and you have it surrounded (the card above and the one below) plus a non-touching higher honour, the best chance of maximum tricks is to lead the card just above dummy's surrounded high card.

Surround position: When you feel that the other three players at the table are all opponents.

Bridge writer: A pen for all seasons.

Quid pro quo: Play for pay.

50 The Count of Del' Monte (Cristo)

The difference between the expert and the average player is the ability and determination to count every hand. Watch expert Ishmael Del'Monte in action on this deal from the 2002 Pacific-Asian Pairs, which he won with Paul Marston.

South dealer : Both vulnerable

```
                North
                ♠ K Q 10 3
                ♡ 9 8 7 6 4
                ◇ - - -
                ♣ 10 9 6 2
West                        East
Del'Monte                   Marston
♠ 9 6 4                     ♠ J 8 7
♡ A Q 2                     ♡ J 10 5 3
◇ 9 8 5 2                   ◇ A K J 4
♣ A 8 5                     ♣ J 3
                South
                ♠ A 5 2
                ♡ K
                ◇ Q 10 7 6 3
                ♣ K Q 7 4
```

West	North	East	South
			1◇
Pass	1♡	Pass	1NT
Pass	Pass	Pass	

West led the ♠6, ten, jack, ace. Declarer returned the ♠5, ♠9, ♠K and ♠8 from East. The ♠8 is the highest remaining spot card in spades. This is consistent with East having started with J-8 or J-8-x. As South would rebid 1♠ with four spades you can place East and South with 3 spades each.

Declarer led the ♣10, jack from East, king from declarer. Del'Monte took this and considered South's shape.

Would South have played clubs like this with K-x-x opposite 10-9-6-2? Hardly. It was more likely that East had J-x and South K-Q-x-x and declarer had planned to run the ♣10. In that case, as South had opened 1◇, South would be 3-2-4-4 or 3-1-5-4.

Tip: *If dummy bids a suit and turns up with a poor holding in that suit, it is often a good idea to lead that suit.* Following that good tip, Del'Monte shifted to the ♡A. The defence took seven tricks to take 1NT down, +100, and 9.5 / 12 matchpoints. A diamond switch would also have worked but this was riskier on the bidding.

'To err is human; to forgive is not winning bridge.'

51   West dealer : Nil vulnerable

              North
              ♠ 7 6
              ♡ K Q 10 9 3
              ◇ K 7 4
              ♣ J 5 2

                         East
                         ♠ 8
                         ♡ 8 6 5 2
                         ◇ A 9 5 2
                         ♣ K 10 9 3

West	North	East	South
1◇	1♡	2◇	3♠
Pass	Pass	Pass	

West leads the ◇Q: king, ace. Plan East's defence.

52   North dealer : North-South vulnerable

              North
              ♠ 10 4
              ♡ Q 9
              ◇ A K Q 8 6
              ♣ Q 10 5 2

                         East
                         ♠ A Q 9 8 2
                         ♡ K 7 5
                         ◇ J 9 7
                         ♣ K 3

West	North	East	South
	1◇	1♠	2♡
2♠	3♣ (1)	Pass	3♡
Pass	4♡	All pass	

(1) Double for takeout is better

West leads the ♠5. Plan the defence for East.

53 North dealer : Both vulnerable

                North
                ♠ K 10 3 2
                ♡ K Q 4 3 2
                ◇ Q
                ♣ 9 7 4

                        East
                        ♠ 7 6 5
                        ♡ A 9 6
                        ◇ A K 9 5
                        ♣ 8 5 2

West	North	East	South	
	Pass	1◇	1NT	
2◇	Dble*	Pass	2NT	*For takeout
Pass	3♡	Pass	3NT	End

Lead: ◇6: Q, K, 2. Switch to ♣8: J, Q, 4. West shifts to the ♠9
to South's ace. South now plays the ♡5: ♡J from West (reverse
count), king from dummy. How should East defend?

54 East dealer : North-South vulnerable

                North
                ♠ A K 6 2
                ♡ 10 6 3
                ◇ A 9 6 4
                ♣ 10 6

                        East
                        ♠ Q J 10 4
                        ♡ Q 4 2
                        ◇ 8 3
                        ♣ K Q J 4

West	North	East	South	
		Pass	1♣*	*3+ clubs
Pass	1♠	Pass	2♠	
Pass	3♠	Pass	3NT	End

West leads ♠5: ♠2, ♠10, ♠7. You, East, switch to the ♣K:
♣2 from South, ♣9 (encouraging) from West. What next?

51 A switch in time

On this deal played on OKbridge, declarer made the contract by fooling West:

West dealer : Nil vulnerable

```
              North
              ♠ 7 6
              ♡ K Q 10 9 3
              ◇ K 7 4
              ♣ J 5 2

West                    East
♠ K 5 4 2               ♠ 8
♡ 7 4                   ♡ 8 6 5 2
◇ Q J 10 3              ◇ A 9 5 2
♣ A Q 6                 ♣ K 10 9 3

              South
              ♠ A Q J 10 9 3
              ♡ A J
              ◇ 8 6
              ♣ 8 7 4
```

West	North	East	South
1◇	1♡	2◇	3♠
Pass	Pass	Pass	

West led the ◇Q, king, ace. East returned a diamond to the ten and declarer ruffed the third diamond. As a club had not been led, declarer deduced that East would hold the ♣Q or ♣K. In that case West was sure to have the ♠K to justify the 1◇ opening.

At trick 4 South led the ♠9, ducked, followed by the ♠A. To give the illusion that he could not reach dummy, declarer cashed the ♡A and continued with the ♠Q, discarding the ♡9 from dummy. West won and, thinking South had no access to dummy, exited with a 'safe' diamond.

Full marks to declarer but none to the defence. A simple count signal by East showing an even number of hearts would give the lie to declarer's holding the ♡A singleton. The real problem comes earlier.

On the bidding, there was at most two diamond tricks for the defence. Likewise, East can see that the defence could not come to more than one trick in hearts. To have any chance of defeating 3♠, there was a need for some tricks from clubs. After winning ◇A at trick 1, East should switch to a club and that takes 3♠ two down.

Deceptive Play: When partner accidentally stumbles on the right move as declarer.

52 The Conscience of the King

North dealer: E-W vulnerable

North
- ♠ 3
- ♡ A J 10 4
- ◇ Q 8 5
- ♣ A K J 10 7

East
- ♠ A 9 7 5
- ♡ 9 7 3
- ◇ K 4
- ♣ 8 6 4 3

South is in 4♡ after 1♣ : 1♡, 3♡ : 4♡. The ♣4 is led to your ace. What next?

There is no hope if South has the ◇A, as dummy's clubs will take care of declarer's losers. Hoping partner has the ◇A, you should shift to the ◇K and hope to ruff the third round of diamonds if declarer began with, say, ◇J-x-x-x.

The same theme was in evidence here from a national pairs event with IMP scoring:

(see deal in next column)

West	North	East	South
	1◇	1♠	2♡
2♠	3♣	Pass	3♡
Pass	4♡	All pass	
Lead: ♠5			

North dealer : N-S vulnerable

North
- ♠ 10 4
- ♡ Q 9
- ◇ A K Q 8 6
- ♣ Q 10 5 2

West
- ♠ J 6 5
- ♡ 10 6
- ◇ 10 5 4 3
- ♣ A 8 7 4

East
- ♠ A Q 9 8 2
- ♡ K 7 5
- ◇ J 9 7
- ♣ K 3

South
- ♠ K 7 3
- ♡ A J 8 4 3 2
- ◇ 2
- ♣ J 9 6

East should take the ♠A and switch to the ♣K. A club to the ace follows and the club ruff means one down. There is little point in pursuing spades. Even if West has the ♠K you cannot come to more than two spade tricks.

You must attack and take your club tricks before declarer can discard them on the diamonds. If South has the ♣A, you had no club tricks coming anyway.

What do bridge players do after a tough day's bridge?
They wine down.

53 The Set-Up

This deal from the final of a major teams event had a number of interesting features:

North dealer : Both vulnerable

```
                North
                ♠ K 10 3 2
                ♡ K Q 4 3 2
                ♢ Q
                ♣ 9 7 4
West                        East
♠ 9 8 4                     ♠ 7 6 5
♡ J 10 8                    ♡ A 9 6
♢ 8 6 4 3                   ♢ A K 9 5
♣ Q 10 3                    ♣ 8 5 2
                South
                ♠ A Q J
                ♡ 7 5
                ♢ J 10 7 2
                ♣ A K J 6
```

West	North	East	South
	Pass	1♢	1NT
2♢	Dble (1)	Pass	2NT
Pass	3♡	Pass	3NT
Pass	Pass	Pass	

(1) For takeout

East opened because of the three quick tricks, but it would be no shame to pass initially. West's raise to 2♢ was quite cavalier. Had South chosen to pass the double for penalties, East would be in –800 territory.

After the ♢6 lead, the bidding and the ♢Q in dummy made it obvious that South had started with ♢J-10-x-x. As there was no point in pursuing diamonds, East won with the ♢K and shifted to ♣8: J – Q – 4.

West switched to the ♠9, ducked to declarer's ace. Back came the ♡5: jack – king – ace. The ♡J could be only from J-10 or J-10-8. Playing reverse count (high-low with an odd number), the J-10-8 holding was the more likely, especially as South had not raised North's 3♡ bid.

East should return the ♡6. That sets up the fifth trick for the defence whether West began with J-10 or J-10-8. If declarer lets the ♡8 hold, West plays a diamond for one down.

The danger for East is to take the ♡A and revert to clubs. Declarer can now win and play the ♢J. This sets up declarer's ninth trick (four spades, three clubs, one heart and one diamond) before the defence can come to a fifth trick.

'Down five': What partner likes to do after each bridge session.

54 To the power of ten

In the final of a national teams championship East did not solve the problem posed on this deal:

East dealer : N-S vulnerable

```
            North
            ♠ A K 6 2
            ♡ 10 6 3
            ◇ A 9 6 4
            ♣ 10 6
West                    East
♠ 5                     ♠ Q J 10 4
♡ K J 9 7               ♡ Q 4 2
◇ J 7 5 2               ◇ 8 3
♣ 9 8 7 5               ♣ K Q J 4
            South
            ♠ 9 8 7 3
            ♡ A 8 5
            ◇ K Q 10
            ♣ A 3 2
```

At one table North-South bid to 3♠ and declarer made nine tricks for +140. At the other:

West	North	East	South
		Pass	1♣ (1)
Pass	1♠	Pass	2♠
Pass	3♠	Pass	3NT
Pass	Pass	Pass	

(1) 3+ clubs

Lead: ♠5

Declarer ducked in dummy and the ♠10 won. East shifted to the ♣K, ♣2 from South and the ♣9, encouraging, from West. East now had to decide whether the ♣9 was from A-9-x, in which case a low club next is best, or from 9-8-x or 9-8-x-x, in which case East should continue with the ♣Q. In practice, East played West for the former and continued with the ♣4. Declarer played low from hand and the ♣10 won.

If West has 4 clubs, the ♣Q next is right. If West has 3 clubs, South has 4 clubs. With a 3-3-3-4 pattern, South is unlikely to raise to 2♠. With 4 spades and 4 clubs, South has a ruffing value in a red suit and would be unlikely to suggest 3NT. That strongly suggests that South is 4-3-3-3 with 4 spades.

Another clue is declarer's play at trick 1. If South is missing the ♣A, would South duck the spade at trick 1? That would give the defence the chance to cash four or more clubs as well as the spade trick. Without the ♣A, South might have ♡A-K-J and ◇K-Q-x in the red suits. If so, South would take the spade trick and try for four tricks in diamonds and three in hearts.

55   Teams : North dealer : Nil vulnerable

               North
               ♠ 7
               ♡ J 5 4
               ◇ A K Q 10 3
               ♣ A 10 9 2
West
♠ A 8 6 3 2
♡ K 6
◇ 8 7
♣ J 8 6 3

West	North	East	South
	1◇	Pass	1♡
Pass	2♣	Pass	3NT
Pass	Pass	Pass	

Lead: ♠3: 7 – Q – K. South plays a diamond to dummy's ace.
Next comes the ♡4: 3 – Q – K. How would you continue as West?

56   Teams : East dealer : Both vulnerable

               North
               ♠ K 7 4 3
               ♡ A J 4
               ◇ K 9 8 4
               ♣ K 7
West
♠ A J 9
♡ Q 7 3
◇ 10 6 2
♣ J 9 4 2

West	North	East	South	
		Pass	1NT*	*11-14, balanced
Pass	2♣	Pass	2◇**	**No 4-card major
Pass	3NT	All pass		

Lead: ♣2: 7 – Q – A. South plays a diamond to dummy's king
and a diamond back to the ace, East playing ◇5, ◇Q. A spade
goes to the king, followed by the ♠3 to the ten and West's jack,
East playing ♠8, ♠6 reverse count. What should West do next?

57   North dealer : North-South vulnerable

            North
            ♠ 9 2
            ♡ Q 10 8 6
            ◇ A 4
            ♣ Q J 8 7 3

West
♠ A 8 7 5
♡ J 4
◇ K 10 5
♣ A 10 5 2

West	North	East	South
	Pass	Pass	1◇
Pass	1♡	Pass	2NT (18-19)
Pass	3NT	All pass	

West leads the ♠5: 2 – 10 – Q. South plays the ♣4: 2 – Q – ◇8 from East. Next the ♣3: ♡7 from East – ♣K – ♣A. East-West play low discard encouraging, high discard discouraging. What should West play at trick 4?

58   South dealer : North-South vulnerable

            North
            ♠ A K J
            ♡ J 10 9 5 3 2
            ◇ K 5
            ♣ A 10

West
♠ Q 5 2
♡ A Q 7 4
◇ 10 4 2
♣ K J 5

West	North	East	South
			Pass
1NT (1)	Dble	Rdble (2)	Pass
2♣	2♡	Pass	3NT
Pass	Pass	Pass	

(1) 11-14 balanced
(2) Asks opener to bid 2♣ but does not promise a club suit

Lead: ♣K, ♣A. East plays the ♣9, reverse signals, discouraging clubs. The ♡J is led from dummy: 6 – 8 – Q. How would you continue as West?

55 The Slender Thread

On this Butler Trials deal, there was no problem in 4♡, but there was a chance to defeat declarer in 3NT.

North dealer : Nil vulnerable

```
              North
              ♠ 7
              ♡ J 5 4
              ◇ A K Q 10 3
              ♣ A 10 9 2
West                        East
♠ A 8 6 3 2                 ♠ Q 10 9 5 4
♡ K 6                       ♡ 10 9 3
◇ 8 7                       ◇ 9 6
♣ J 8 6 3                   ♣ K 5 4
              South
              ♠ K J
              ♡ A Q 8 7 2
              ◇ J 5 4 2
              ♣ Q 7
```

West	North	East	South
	1◇	Pass	1♡
Pass	2♣	Pass	3NT
Pass	Pass	Pass	

Lead: ♠3

A better sequence would be 1◇ : 1♡, 2♡ : 4♡. In 4♡, declarer loses at most one spade, one heart and one club.

Against 3NT, West leads a low spade to the queen and king. A diamond to dummy is followed by a low heart to the queen and king. West can place South with the A-Q in hearts, for East would have risen with the ♡A to return a spade.

The temptation is to switch to a club to try to put East on lead to play a spade through declarer. That cannot work if you count declarer's winners. On obtaining the lead, declarer figures to have nine tricks via five diamonds, two hearts, one spade and one club or perhaps three diamonds, four hearts, one spade and one club.

At teams your aim is to beat the contract. To do that West needs to play the ♠A in the hope that declarer started with ♠K-J doubleton. That is a slender chance, but the only one.

The meek may inherit the earth but they lose at bridge.

Vulnerability: The excuse used when bidding too little when vulnerable and too much when not vulnerable.

LHO = left-hand opponent.
RHO = right-hand opponent.
MHO = middle-hand opponent.

56 The switching hour

East-West did well on this deal from a Butler Trials event (pairs with IMP-scoring):

East dealer : Both vulnerable

```
              North
              ♠ K 7 4 3
              ♡ A J 4
              ◇ K 9 8 4
              ♣ K 7
West                        East
♠ A J 9                     ♠ 8 6 5
♡ Q 7 3                     ♡ K 10 8 6 2
◇ 10 6 2                    ◇ Q 5
♣ J 9 4 2                   ♣ Q 8 3
              South
              ♠ Q 10 2
              ♡ 9 5
              ◇ A J 7 3
              ♣ A 10 6 5
```

West	North	East	South
		Pass	1NT
Pass	2♣	Pass	2◇ (1)
Pass	3NT	All pass	

(1) No 4-card major

Lead: ♣2

East's ♣Q was taken by the ace. Declarer continued with a diamond to the king and a diamond back, capturing East's ◇Q *en route*. Next came the ♠2 to the king and a spade back to the ten and jack.

Had West woodenly played a 'safe' club, declarer has nine tricks by simply playing another spade. West switched to a low heart, ducked to East's ten and East returned a low heart to West's ♡Q.

Declarer should duck this for one down (West switches to the low club if the ♡Q holds), but took the ♡A. West won the spade exit and played another heart to take 3NT two down. That was worth +200 and +9 Imps as the datum (or average) was North-South 210.

As declarer needs spade tricks anyway, South might have played a spade to the king at trick 2, followed by a spade to the ten and jack. With the diamond position not yet revealed, West might play a club at trick 4. A third spade will then be enough to give declarer nine tricks.

Viewgraph: Opportunity given to two or three experts to take turns at making mistakes in analysis.

Precision Bidding: A contradiction in terms.

57 Mind reader

On this deal from a bridge session on the internet, East tried to send a vital message, but to no avail.

North dealer : N-S vulnerable

```
            North
            ♠ 9 2
            ♡ Q 10 8 6
            ◇ A 4
            ♣ Q J 8 7 3
West                    East
♠ A 8 7 5               ♠ J 10 6 4 3
♡ J 4                   ♡ 9 7 5 3 2
◇ K 10 5                ◇ 8 3 2
♣ A 10 5 2              ♣ - - -
            South
            ♠ K Q
            ♡ A K
            ◇ Q J 9 7 6
            ♣ K 9 6 4
```

West	North	East	South
	Pass	Pass	1◇
Pass	1♡	Pass	2NT
Pass	3NT	All pass	

Lead: ♠5

East followed with the ♠10 and South won with the ♠Q. Declarer played the ♣4 to the queen and East discarded the ◇8 (playing high-discouraging). This was followed by the ♣3 to South's king and West's ace. This time East pitched the ♡7, another high discouraging card.

It was now up to West to find the killing continuation. When West exited with a 'safe' club, it was a killing move, but only for the defence's prospects. The winning play was to lay down the ♠A and thus take four spades and the ♣A.

You would not need to be a mind reader to work out that East wants spades. East's red suit discards say, 'I do not want diamonds. I do not want hearts. I do not have clubs. Guess what I do want?'

There is another clue, too. At trick 1 South played the ♠Q, letting West know that South had the ♠K as well. Why would South be so generous in handing over this information? Only if South did not want the spades continued later.

The position should have been clear to West, but maybe it would have been clearer with McKenney discards, the ◇8 and the ♡9 asking for the high suit each time. Odd-card-encourage, even suit-preference would also do it. Using this method, East discards the ◇8, then the ◇2, asking West to play spades.

58 A bad hand for the count

This deal is from the final of a national teams championship:

South dealer : N-S vulnerable

```
              North
              ♠ A K J
              ♡ J 10 9 5 3 2
              ◇ K 5
              ♣ A 10

West                        East
♠ Q 5 2                     ♠ 9 8 6 3
♡ A Q 7 4                   ♡ 6
◇ 10 4 2                    ◇ A J 9 8 7
♣ K J 5                     ♣ 9 6 3

              South
              ♠ 10 7 4
              ♡ K 8
              ◇ Q 6 3
              ♣ Q 8 7 4 2
```

West	North	East	South
			Pass
1NT	Dble	Rdble	Pass
2♣	2♡	Pass	3NT
Pass	Pass	Pass	

1NT was 11-14 balanced. The redouble was the beginning of a rescue operation and did not promise club length. East was planning to remove 2♣ to 2◇.

Declarer took the ♣K lead with the ace and ran the ♡J to the queen. West did not find the diamond shift and declarer made ten tricks for +630 and +10 Imps to North-South.

If playing attitude signals on partner's lead, East should discourage clubs at trick 1 (♣3 if playing high encourage, ♣9 with reverse signals). When in with the ♡Q, West should now find the diamond shift to defeat 3NT. East cannot want spades or hearts and has discouraged clubs.

Declarer has no successful play on the diamond switch. If the ◇K is played from dummy, East wins and plays a second diamond. South has to duck. East then needs to revert to clubs to defeat the contract. That would not be too tough.

Note how useless count signals are here. If East signals on the ♣K to show an odd number of clubs, West does not know if this is three or five. West does not want or need count here. What West needs to know is whether to pursue clubs or switch to diamonds. An attitude signal is needed.

Note also that despite the 6-2 fit in hearts, 4♡ has four losers while 3NT made in practice.

PART 5: Improve Your Declarer Play

59   Teams : South dealer : North-South vulnerable

North
- ♠ A 9 4 3
- ♡ 6 5 2
- ◇ 7 5 3 2
- ♣ A 8

South
- ♠ Q 5
- ♡ A Q 4
- ◇ - - -
- ♣ Q J 10 9 6 4 3 2

South opens 5♣ and everyone passes. West leads the ◇K. Plan the play.

60   Teams : North dealer : North-South vulnerable

North
- ♠ K Q 10
- ♡ K 10
- ◇ K 9 7 5
- ♣ J 4 3 2

West	North	East	South
	1NT (1)	Dble (2)	2♡
Dble (2)	Pass	Pass	Pass
(1) 12-14			
(2) Penalties			

South
- ♠ J 5
- ♡ A 9 7 5 3
- ◇ J 10 8 4 3
- ♣ 10

West led the ◇Q, king, ace. East switched to the ♣K and West discouraged with the ♣5. East reverted to the ◇6, ruffed by West, who shifted to the ♠2, king, ace. West ruffed the diamond return and tried the ♣A.

South ruffed the ♣A and played a low heart: queen, king, two. Next came the ♡10: ♡8 from East. What do you play from hand?

61   Teams : East dealer : Nil vulnerable

North
- ♠ A K Q 6 5 4
- ♡ - - -
- ◇ K J 9
- ♣ J 10 8 6

South
- ♠ - - -
- ♡ K Q 9 7 6 5 4 3
- ◇ - - -
- ♣ A Q 9 7 2

South is in 4♡, no opposition bidding. West leads the ◇A, ruffed, and you play the ♡K, ♡8 from West. East wins and shifts to the ♣4. Plan the play.

62   Pairs : West dealer : Nil vulnerable

North
- ♠ J 6
- ♡ A 7 3
- ◇ Q J 10 6 4
- ♣ 9 8 3

South
- ♠ Q 4
- ♡ K J 10
- ◇ 9 8 2
- ♣ A K J 6 2

West	North	East	South
1♠	Pass	2♠	3♣
Pass	Pass	Pass	

West leads the ◇A, East plays ◇7 (high card encouraging). What should South play on that?

West shifts to the ♠10, won by East with the ace. Back comes the ♡4 and South's ♡J holds the trick. How would you continue?

59 Classy Play

This deal arose in a qualifying round of a national teams event:

South dealer : N-S vulnerable

```
                North
                ♠ A 9 4 3
                ♡ 6 5 2
                ◇ 7 5 3 2
                ♣ A 8
West                        East
♠ 10 7 6                    ♠ K J 8 2
♡ K 10 8 3                  ♡ J 9 7
◇ K Q J 6                   ◇ A 10 9 8 4
♣ K 5                       ♣ 7
                South
                ♠ Q 5
                ♡ A Q 4
                ◇ - - -
                ♣ Q J 10 9 6 4 3 2
```

West	North	East	South
			5♣
Pass	Pass	Pass	

Lead: ◇K

After ruffing the ◇K, South should try to benefit from a favourable location of the ♠K, the ♡K and / or the ♣K. The winning line is to play a low club and finesse dummy's ♣8. When that wins, continue with a low spade to your queen. If the queen were to lose to the king, you would need to fall back on the heart finesse.

If East plays low, the ♠Q will win and the contract is safe. In practice, East will rise with the ♠K. If East now shifts to a heart you must rise with the ♡A, cash the ♠Q and lead a club to dummy's ace. You can then discard a heart on the ♠A.

When East plays a heart after winning with the ♠K, it would be an error to finesse the ♡Q. West would win and the ♣K would then eliminate your entry to dummy with the spades still blocked.

'Indiscretion': A term applied to your inferior choice, which would be labelled a blunder if committed by partner.

'Smother play': A highly attractive move against your partner after each session.

Squeezed in the majors: A very painful experience.
Squeezed in the minors: Almost as painful as being squeezed in the majors.

Something to say to your partner: 'If you had as good a partner as I have, we'd be in great shape.'

60 The Running Man

This deal comes from the final of the Grand National Open Teams:

Dealer North : N-S vulnerable

```
            North
            ♠ K Q 10
            ♡ K 10
            ◇ K 9 7 5
            ♣ J 4 3 2
West                    East
♠ 9 8 6 4 2             ♠ A 7 3
♡ Q 6 4                 ♡ J 8 2
◇ Q                     ◇ A 6 2
♣ A 8 7 5              ♣ K Q 9 6
            South
            ♠ J 5
            ♡ A 9 7 5 3
            ◇ J 10 8 4 3
            ♣ 10
```

West	North	East	South
	1NT (1)	Dble	2♡
Dble	Pass	Pass	Pass

(1) 12-14

Lead: ◇Q

Both doubles were for penalties.

No doubt North-South have methods to show two-suiters and so running to 2♡ was a calculated risk. West, Ishmael Del'Monte, led the ◇Q, king, ace. East switched to the ♣K and West discouraged with the ♣5. East reverted to the ◇6,

ruffed by West, who switched to the ♠2, king, ace. West ruffed the diamond return and tried the ♣A.

South ruffed and played a heart: queen, king, two. Next came the ♡10: eight . . . and South had to decide the heart layout. Ultimately he rose with the ♡A, playing West to have doubled 2♡ with Q-J-6-4. When the ♡J did not fall, declarer was one down, –200.

It is certainly more likely that West would have ♡Q-J-x-x than ♡Q-x-x to double for penalties, but there are slight clues pointing the other way. With ♡Q-J-x-x, would West be leading ◇Q singleton, seeking a ruff? Would West not be more likely to lead a long suit to try for a forcing defence? The short suit lead is more likely to suggest three trumps than four.

Still, the blame for the outcome is less on the declarer play than on the failure to locate the diamond fit. At the other table North-South scored +130 in 3◇ by North.

61 Freak out

An 8-5 pattern is a rarity. This one arose in the qualifying rounds of a selection event:

East dealer : Nil vulnerable

```
              North
              ♠ A K Q 6 5 4
              ♡ - - -
              ◇ K J 9
              ♣ J 10 8 6
West                      East
♠ J 7 2                   ♠ 10 9 8 3
♡ 8                       ♡ A J 10 2
◇ A Q 8 7 4 3             ◇ 10 6 5 2
♣ K 5 3                   ♣ 4
              South
              ♠ - - -
              ♡ K Q 9 7 6 5 4 3
              ◇ - - -
              ♣ A Q 9 7 2
```

At one table the bidding went:

West	North	East	South
		Pass	6♡
Pass	Pass	Pass	

East chose a good moment not to open 2◇ to show a weak hand with both majors. East declined to double 6♡ lest South have an escape to 6NT. Opening 6♡ might work on some days. This was not one of them. Three down.

You can afford to open with a one-bid when you have a freak hand with a low high card count. The bidding will not die out at the one-level. Opening 1♡ does allow the opposition in cheaply but it gives you room to discover how the land lies. There were many 2♣ and 2◇ openings, but these are misguided with so few points. If you encounter interference you have no chance of showing your hand type.

One South scored a triumph by opening a modest 4♡. The ◇A was led, ruffed, and the ♡K was taken by East who switched to the ♣4. Declarer rose with the ♣A and continued with ♡Q and a third heart. With no more clubs, East had to give the lead to dummy and declarer's clubs vanished on the ◇K and top spades. As the median was 50 to E-W, making 4♡ was worth 10 Imps.

'Laydown': A term that is never applied to a contract where partner is declarer.

Real men don't show two-suiters.

62 Adding to success

South made full use of a slip by the defence on this deal from a major pairs event:

West dealer : Nil vulnerable

```
        North
        ♠ J 6
        ♡ A 7 3
        ◇ Q J 10 6 4
        ♣ 9 8 3
West              East
♠ K 10 9 7 5      ♠ A 8 3 2
♡ 8 5 2           ♡ Q 9 6 4
◇ A K 5           ◇ 7 3
♣ Q 7             ♣ 10 5 4
        South
        ♠ Q 4
        ♡ K J 10
        ◇ 9 8 2
        ♣ A K J 6 2
```

West	North	East	South
1♠	Pass	2♠	3♣
Pass	Pass	Pass	

Opening lead: ◇A

East-West did well in the bidding since 3♠ is one down and 3♣ can be defeated. West led the ◇A and East played the ◇7, an encouraging signal. South followed carefully with the ◇2. Had he played the ◇8 or ◇9, East's signal would be obvious to West. With the appearance of the ◇2, West thought the ◇7 might be lowest from 9-8-7, discouraging, and a second diamond would set up winners for declarer.

West shifted to a low spade to the ace. East could now return the ◇3 for the ruff, but he felt that West's failure to continue diamonds indicated a 4-card suit. As a diamond return would then set up dummy's diamonds, East switched to a low heart to try to knock out the ♡A entry to the diamonds.

South played the ♡J, which won the trick. He now did a little arithmetic. Of the 18 HCP missing, East had turned up with six. West would therefore have the rest to justify the opening bid and so declarer continued with ♣A and ♣K. When the ♣Q fell, he drew the last trump and had nine tricks for +110 and a huge score.

Understanding bridge jargon: 'Three of the boards are worth examining.' = 'I had bad results on the others.'

'Typical results are the following:' = 'My best results are the following:'

63 Pairs : South dealer : North-South vulnerable

North
- ♠ Q 6 2
- ♡ K 8 7 5 4 2
- ◇ K Q 10
- ♣ 8

South
- ♠ K 10 8 5
- ♡ A Q J 10 6
- ◇ A 8 7
- ♣ 4

West	North	East	South
			1♡
1♠	4♡	5♣	Pass
Pass	5♡	All pass	

West leads the ♣A and switches to the ◇4. Plan the play.

64 Pairs : South dealer : North-South vulnerable

North
- ♠ Q J 7
- ♡ Q J 4 3
- ◇ K 8 3 2
- ♣ A 4

South
- ♠ A K 9 6 4
- ♡ A 8 7 5
- ◇ 6 5
- ♣ K 9

West	North	East	South
			1♠
Pass	2◇	Pass	2♡
Pass	4♡	All pass	

West leads the ◇Q, ducked, and continues with the ◇J, ducked again in dummy. East takes with the ace and switches to a low club. Plan the play.

65   Pairs : South dealer : Nil vulnerable

North
- ♠ 8 5 4
- ♡ K 4 3 2
- ◇ A 10 5 3
- ♣ A 10

South
- ♠ A K Q J 6 3
- ♡ Q 5
- ◇ 6 4
- ♣ J 8 6

West	North	East	South
			1♠
Pass	2◇	Pass	2♠
Pass	4♠	All pass	

West leads the ◇Q. Plan the play.

66   Teams : East dealer : East-West vulnerable

North
- ♠ Q 7 4
- ♡ 10
- ◇ A K 5 2
- ♣ K Q 6 5 3

West	North	East	South
		2◇ (1)	Pass
2♡	Dble	Pass	3♣
Pass	Pass	Pass	

(1) 11-15 points, 5+ hearts and 4+ spades

South
- ♠ A 8 3
- ♡ Q 9 6 3
- ◇ 9 4 3
- ♣ J 9 7

Lead: ♡5 – 10 – K – 3. East returns ◇10, won by the ace. On the
♣3 East takes the ♣A and continues with ◇6, won by the king.
On the next diamond, East discards a heart and West wins. West
shifts to the ♠5, low from dummy, ♠J from East. Plan the play.

63 Coup de Grace

At a Pro-Am session with ten experts partnering average club members, one East-West found the killing defence on this deal, which prevented declarer from finding a very pretty play.

South dealer : N-S vulnerable

```
              North
              ♠ Q 6 2
              ♡ K 8 7 5 4 2
              ◇ K Q 10
              ♣ 8

West                     East
♠ A J 7 4 3              ♠ 9
♡ 9                      ♡ 3
◇ 9 4 3 2                ◇ J 6 5
♣ A 6 5                  ♣ K Q J 10 9 7 3 2

              South
              ♠ K 10 8 5
              ♡ A Q J 10 6
              ◇ A 8 7
              ♣ 4
```

South opens 1♡, West bids 1♠, North makes some raise in hearts and East offers 5♣. The winning decision is to double 5♣ for +300, but many pairs went on to 5♡.

Declarer had no chance when West led the ♠A and another spade, ruffed. East shifted to a club for one down.

At other tables West started with the ♣A and shifted to a diamond. With the spade layout almost certain because of the overcall, declarer should draw trumps and then eliminate the diamonds. The *coup de grace* is the ♠K. Whether West takes this or ducks, declarer loses only one spade trick.

If you bid 5-over-5 you had better be right, lucky or play well.

Tips for bridge writers:
  Always avoid all alliteration.
  Avoid cliches like the plague.
  Be more or less specific.
  One should never generalize.
  Proofread carefully to see if you any words out.
  Never use a long word when a diminutive one will do.
  Don't be redundant; don't use more words than necessary; you do not need to do that; it is most superfluous.
  Always try to eschew ampersands & abbreviations, etc.
  Be sure to never split an infinitive.
  The passive voice is to be avoided.
  Understatement is always best.
  Avoid parenthetical observations (no matter how relevant).
  Be careful because it is very easy to misuse apostrophe's.

64 The Tender Trap

Ishmael Del'Monte – Paul Marston did well on this deal *en route* to winning the 2002 Pacific-Asian Pairs.

South dealer : N-S vulnerable

```
            North
            Marston
            ♠ Q J 7
            ♡ Q J 4 3
            ◇ K 8 3 2
            ♣ A 4
West                      East
♠ 10 8                    ♠ 5 3 2
♡ K 10                    ♡ 9 6 2
◇ Q J 10 9 7              ◇ A 4
♣ 10 7 5 2                ♣ Q J 8 6 3
            South
            Del'Monte
            ♠ A K 9 6 4
            ♡ A 8 7 5
            ◇ 6 5
            ♣ K 9
```

Via a relay auction North-South reached 4♡ with South declarer. West led the ◇Q, ducked, and continued with the ◇J, ducked again in dummy. East won with the ace perforce and switched to a low club.

The percentage play with this trump combination is a low heart towards dummy. This holds the trump losers to one whenever trumps are 3-2, if West has ♡K-x-x-x or a singleton ♡K, ♡10 or ♡9. A number of declarers failed the test when they won the club exit and started trumps by playing ♡A and another heart. West won the second heart and played a third diamond. Dummy had to follow and East was able to ruff with the ♡9 for one down.

Realizing the inherent danger, Del'Monte avoided this trap. He won the third club with the king and led a low heart. West took the ♡K, but declarer could over-ruff East on the third diamond and draw trumps for +420.

Understanding bridge jargon:
'Although the hand records do not provide details, it is clear from the result that . . .' = 'It is impossible to tell how this result could possibly have been achieved.'

'This event will be reported in a later issue.' = 'I might get around to writing this sometime.'

'Correct on most layouts' = 'Wrong.'

'The team can do better.' = 'It could hardly do worse.'

65 Caught in the slips

Declarer slipped up on this deal from the final of a national pairs championship.

South dealer : Nil vulnerable

North
♠ 8 5 4
♡ K 4 3 2
◇ A 10 5 3
♣ A 10

West
♠ 10 9 7 2
♡ A J 6
◇ Q J 2
♣ Q 7 5

East
♠ - - -
♡ 10 9 8 7
◇ K 9 8 7
♣ K 9 4 3 2

South
♠ A K Q J 6 3
♡ Q 5
◇ 6 4
♣ J 8 6

West	North	East	South
			1♠
Pass	2◇	Pass	2♠
Pass	4♠	All pass	

Lead: ◇Q

With 3-card support and a ruffing value, together with 11 HCP consisting of two aces and a king, North was easily worth the raise to 4♠.

The ◇A took trick 1. Ten tricks look routine and that is when one must beware. What could go wrong?

The successful play is straightforward. Cash the ♣A at trick 2 and play a second club. On regaining the lead, ruff the club loser in dummy and draw trumps. As three losers are virtually inevitable after the diamond lead, there is no reason to shun this play.

In practice declarer played a low heart to his queen at trick 2. This seems innocuous, but look what happened. West captured the ♡Q and continued with the ◇J and a third diamond. South ruffed and led a club to the ten and king. East returned the ◇K and West now made a trump trick. One down.

According to an evening paper, there are only five real authorities on bridge . . . Odd how often one gets one of them as a partner. ('Punch' magazine).

'Ace': A card that despite everyone's expectations never takes more than one trick (and sometimes not even that).

'Alcatraz Coup': Normal outcome of a hold-up play using a double-barrelled Stayman.

66 'Information, how can I help you?'

Les Longhurst represented Australia in the 1976 world championships after winning the 1975 Open Trials easily. On this deal from the Butler Trials, he made the most of the information from the auction:

West dealer : E-W vulnerable

```
           North
           ♠ Q 7 4
           ♡ 10
           ◇ A K 5 2
           ♣ K Q 6 5 3
West              East
♠ 10 6 5          ♠ K J 9 2
♡ J 7 5           ♡ A K 8 4 2
◇ Q J 8 7         ◇ 10 6
♣ 10 8 2          ♣ A 4
           South
           Longhurst
           ♠ A 8 3
           ♡ Q 9 6 3
           ◇ 9 4 3
           ♣ J 9 7
```

Contract: 3♣ after East opened 2◇ (4 spades, 5+ hearts).

West led the ♡5: 10 – K – 3 and the ◇10 came back, taken by the ace. On the low club lead from dummy, East did well to rise with the ♣A, else he could soon be endplayed.

East exited with his second diamond, won by the king. Needing to ruff dummy's fourth diamond in hand, Longhurst led a third diamond, taken by West. On the ♠5 shift (the ♠10 is better), South played low from dummy and ducked East's jack.

East played the ♣4, the only safe exit, but Longhurst was in complete control. After ruffing the ♡6, he ruffed dummy's last diamond with the ♣9 and ruffed another heart with dummy's ♣Q, leaving:

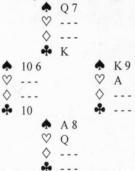

```
           ♠ Q 7
           ♡ - - -
           ◇ - - -
           ♣ K
♠ 10 6            ♠ K 9
♡ - - -           ♡ A
◇ - - -           ◇ - - -
♣ 10              ♣ - - -
           ♠ A 8
           ♡ Q
           ◇ - - -
           ♣ - - -
```

When Longhurst played the ♣K to draw the last trump, East was squeezed in the majors.

Friends are like stars . . . you do not always see them, but you know they are there.

Realist: Someone who knows the pessimist is right.

67   Pairs : West dealer : Both vulnerable

North
♠ 10 7 6 4 2
♡ K J 5 3
♢ 9 4
♣ K 6

South
♠ A
♡ A Q 6
♢ A Q J 10 6 2
♣ Q 5 4

West	North	East	South
1♠	Pass	Pass	3NT
Pass	Pass	Pass	

West leads the ♡10. Plan the play.

68   East dealer : Nil vulnerable

North
♠ K 6 3 2
♡ K J 6 5
♢ K 8 4
♣ 7 6

South
♠ 9 7
♡ A Q 10 8 4 3
♢ A J 7
♣ J 8

West	North	East	South
		Pass	1♡
Dble	3♢ (1)	Pass	4♡
Pass	Pass	Pass	

(1) 10-12 points, 4+ hearts

West leads the ♣2 and East takes ♣K, ♣A before switching to
♠4 to West's ace. West continues with ♠Q. Plan the play.

69   South dealer : North-South vulnerable

> North
> ♠ A 9 4
> ♡ A 8 4
> ◇ A K J 10 9
> ♣ K Q
>
> South
> ♠ J 5 3
> ♡ K 6
> ◇ Q 2
> ♣ A 10 9 6 4 3

South is in 7♣ on the ♡3 lead, won by the ♡K. You play off the ♣K, ♣Q. West follows once, then discards the ♡2. Plan the play.

70   East dealer : Nil vulnerable

> North
> ♠ A
> ♡ A 9 8 5 4
> ◇ 10 6 3
> ♣ 7 6 5 4
>
> South
> ♠ K J 10
> ♡ K J 10 3 2
> ◇ A 9 7 2
> ♣ 3

West	North	East	South
		1♣	1♡
1♠	4♡	4♠	5♡
Pass	Pass	Pass	

West leads the ♣8. East wins with the ♣K and continues with the ♣A. Plan the play.

67 Duck Soup

There are several internet bridge clubs which allow you to play 24 hours a day, 365 days a year. This deal comes from a match-pointed pairs game on the 'net:

West dealer : Both vulnerable

```
              North
              ♠ 10 7 6 4 2
              ♡ K J 5 3
              ◇ 9 4
              ♣ K 6
West                        East
♠ K Q 8 5 3                 ♠ J 9
♡ 10 9 8 4                  ♡ 7 2
◇ K 7                       ◇ 8 5 3
♣ A 8                       ♣ J 10 9 7 3 2
              South
              ♠ A
              ♡ A Q 6
              ◇ A Q J 10 6 2
              ♣ Q 5 4
```

West	North	East	South
1♠	Pass	Pass	3NT
Pass	Pass	Pass	

West's failure to lead a spade meant that the spades were not headed by ♠K-Q-J and so East had to have at least the ♠J. As only 14 HCP were missing, South quickly deduced that the ◇K had to be with West.

At teams you would tackle diamonds to make sure of your contract. At pairs, you have ten tricks but should you try for eleven? It could be sensible to settle for ten since a spade lead might have held you to nine tricks. Also, some pairs may not be in game or may reach 4♡, which might make just ten tricks.

West is unlikely to duck with ◇K-x if you play a low diamond, but a duck with ♣A-x or ♣A-x-x is more natural. Declarer won the ♡10 lead in hand and played a low club at trick 2. The risk is that West rises with the ♣A and shifts to a spade, possibly limiting you to nine tricks. As West did not lead a spade initially, it is unlikely that West will now see the urgency to play a spade.

West did play low on the club and dummy's king won. South continued with a diamond to the ace and another diamond, making eleven tricks for +660. This was worth 97% of the match-points. Playing safe for ten tricks would also have been a good score, 85%.

68 Counted Out

As soon as dummy appears, count the HCP in dummy. Add them to those in your hand and deduct the total from 40 to see how many points are missing. If there has been opposition bidding, you can often tell where the missing strength lies after a trick or two.

East dealer : Nil vulnerable

```
              North
              ♠ K 6 3 2
              ♡ K J 6 5
              ◇ K 8 4
              ♣ 7 6
West                      East
♠ A Q J 5                 ♠ 10 8 4
♡ 2                       ♡ 9 7
◇ Q 9 6 5                 ◇ 10 3 2
♣ Q 10 4 2                ♣ A K 9 5 3
              South
              ♠ 9 7
              ♡ A Q 10 8 4 3
              ◇ A J 7
              ♣ J 8
```

West	North	East	South
		Pass	1♡
Dble	3◇ (1)	Pass	4♡
Pass	Pass	Pass	

(1) 10-12 points, 4+ hearts

Lead: ♣2

After ♣K, ♣A, East shifted to the ♠4. West won with the ♠A and continued with ♠Q.

Declarer has lost three tricks and at first blush the contract seems to depend on the diamond finesse, which fails.

A count of HCP with declarer and dummy comes to 22. That leaves 18. East has turned up with 7. The other 11 should all be with West to justify the takeout double and so you know the diamond finesse will lose.

Win ♠K, play ♡A, ♡K, ruff the third round of spades and then continue hearts. Almost certain to hold four spades on the auction, West will be squeezed in spades and diamonds. This will be the position with one trump to go:

```
              ♠ 6
              ◇ K 8 4
♠ J                      ◇ 10 3 2
◇ Q 9 6                  ♣ 9
              ♡ 8
              ◇ A J 7
```

Declarer plays the ♡8 and West must let go a diamond, else dummy's ♠6 is high. Now ◇K and ◇A fells the queen and the contract is home.

Should husbands and wives play bridge together?
Not if they want to stay married.

69 Reduction leads to success

Trump reduction technique is the key to success on this deal:

South dealer : N-S vulnerable

```
              North
              ♠ A 9 4
              ♡ A 8 4
              ◇ A K J 10 9
              ♣ K Q
West                      East
♠ K 8 7 2                 ♠ Q 10 6
♡ 9 7 5 3 2               ♡ Q J 10
◇ 8 7 3                   ◇ 6 5 4
♣ 8                       ♣ J 7 5 2
              South
              ♠ J 5 3
              ♡ K 6
              ◇ Q 2
              ♣ A 10 9 6 4 3
```

The play in 7♣, 7◇ and 7NT would be trivial if the clubs behaved. With East holding ♣J-x-x-x, 7NT and 7◇ are hopeless but 7♣ is still viable.

The ♡3 lead is won by the ♡K, and the ♣K, ♣Q reveal the bad break. Time for trump reduction. Continue with a heart to the ace and ruff a heart. Now play four rounds of diamonds, discarding your spade losers.

If East ruffs the diamond, you over-ruff, draw the last trump and claim. If East discards a spade, play the fifth diamond and ruff it, even though it is high. You must bring your trump length down to the same as East's. This will be the ending:

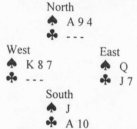

```
              North
              ♠ A 9 4
              ♣ - - -
West                      East
♠ K 8 7                   ♠ Q
♣ - - -                   ♣ J 7
              South
              ♠ J
              ♣ A 10
```

Declarer plays a spade to the ace and has the last two tricks.

No one reached a grand slam on the above deal and many missed even a small slam. The deal arose in a pairs event with IMP-scoring.

Datums (averages): Open 1110, Women's 1100, Seniors 1220.

Open: 4 bid 6♣, 4 bid 6NT and six stopped lower.

Women's: 4 in 6NT, 2 in 6♣ and 5 in game.

Seniors: 1 in 6NT, 4 in 6♣ and 2 in game.

'Winning line: The play discovered by three or more players after two hours of post-mortem and which should have been found by declarer after two minutes.'

70 Asleep at the wheel

Take a look at the odd play on this deal from the final of a national teams championship:

East dealer : Nil vulnerable

```
              North
              ♠ A
              ♡ A 9 8 5 4
              ◇ 10 6 3
              ♣ 7 6 5 4
West                      East
♠ 9 8 6 5 4              ♠ Q 7 3 2
♡ 7                      ♡ Q 6
◇ K J 8 4                ◇ Q 5
♣ Q 9 8                  ♣ A K J 10 2
              South
              ♠ K J 10
              ♡ K J 10 3 2
              ◇ A 9 7 2
              ♣ 3
```

West	North	East	South
		1♣	1♡
1♠	4♡	4♠	5♡
Pass	Pass	Pass	

Lead: ♣8

The contract was the same at both tables. East won with the ♣K and continued with the ♣A. How should South play?

This looks like a stroll in the park: ruff the club, play a heart to the ace, cash the ♠A and draw the last trump with a heart to the king. After discarding a diamond from dummy on the ♠K, you can claim, ruffing two more clubs in hand and losing just one club and one diamond.

This is just a matter of counting your tricks: two spades, two top hearts and six ruffs make ten tricks and the ◇A is eleven. The deal would be too simple for a novice-intermediate text-book but look what happened in practice.

One declarer miscounted her tricks and went one down. As this book might find its way into the hands of children, declarer's line of play cannot be revealed, lest it lead to nightmares.

At the other table, the contract made despite declarer's efforts: ♣K wins; ♣A ruffed; ♡J to the ace. Fine so far. Next came club ruff with ♡3; ♠10 to the ace; ♣7 ruffed with the ♡10 (phew, no over-ruff) and finally the ♡K was cashed.

'Reversal of fortune': When partner actually makes a hand as declarer.

71   North dealer : Both vulnerable

North
♠ 8 3
♡ K 10 9 5 4 3
♢ K 8
♣ 9 8 7

South
♠ A Q 7
♡ Q 8 6 2
♢ A 7 3
♣ K Q 3

West	North	East	South
	Pass	Pass	1NT
Pass	2◇ (1)	Pass	3♡(2)
Pass	4♡	All pass	

(1) Transfer to hearts   (2) Maximum 1NT with four hearts

West leads the ♣6: 7 – 10 – king. Plan the play.

72   West dealer : East-West vulnerable

North
♠ Q 8 7
♡ Q 10 8 5
♢ A K 3
♣ Q 4 3

South
♠ A J 10 6 4 3 2
♡ A 9 6 3
♢ - - -
♣ 7 5

West	North	East	South
Pass	1♣	1NT	4♠
Pass	Pass	Pass	

West leads the ♣J, ducked all round. East takes the next club with the king and continues with the ♣A. Plan the play.

73   West dealer : North-South vulnerable

> North
> ♠ K 7
> ♡ A Q 2
> ◇ Q 7 5 2
> ♣ K Q 9 3
>
> South
> ♠ A Q 10 9 4 2
> ♡ 10 5 4
> ◇ A 8
> ♣ A 4

6♠ by South, no E-W bidding. West leads the ◇J: 2 – 3 – ace.
You draw trumps in three rounds, West discarding a heart on the
third spade. How do you continue?

74   Teams : South dealer : East-West vulnerable

> North
> ♠ K 10 6
> ♡ A Q 8
> ◇ A J 9 3
> ♣ A Q J
>
> South
> ♠ A Q 9
> ♡ 9 7 6 2
> ◇ K Q 7
> ♣ K 8 3

West	North	East	South
			1NT
Pass	6NT	All pass	

West leads the ♣6. Plan the play.

71 Shutting the exits

This deal arose in a national teams championship:

North dealer : Both vulnerable

```
            North
            ♠ 8 3
            ♡ K 10 9 5 4 3
            ◇ K 8
            ♣ 9 8 7
West                    East
♠ K 10 9 5 4            ♠ J 6 2
♡ A 7                   ♡ J
◇ Q 10 9 5              ◇ J 6 4 2
♣ 6 2                   ♣ A J 10 5 4
            South
            ♠ A Q 7
            ♡ Q 8 6 2
            ◇ A 7 3
            ♣ K Q 3
```

West	North	East	South
	Pass	Pass	1NT
Pass	2◇ (1)	Pass	3♡ (2)
Pass	4♡	All pass	

(1) Transfer to hearts
(2) Maximum 1NT, four hearts

West led the ♣6: 7 – 10 – king. The ♣6 was the highest spot card and therefore a singleton or top of a doubleton. East did well to duck the first club. If East takes the ♣A and returns a club, there is no defence.

The temptation for declarer on winning the club lead is to play a trump at once. If you do, West wins, plays a second club to East's ace and scores a club ruff. West exits with a diamond and you later lose a spade trick for one down.

Spotting the danger of a club ruff (why else would East not take the ♣A at once?), declarer eliminated the diamonds before touching trumps: ◇K, ◇A, diamond ruff. Now a trump was led to the queen and ace.

West reverted to clubs. East took the ace and gave West a club ruff, but West was endplayed. Forced into leading a spade or giving declarer a ruff-and-discard, West had to eliminate South's spade loser one way or another and the contract was made.

The police covered all the exits. Unluckily the thieves escaped through an entrance.

Third hand play at trick 1: The second chance for the defence to blunder.

Reverse signal: Partner takes the signal to mean the opposite of what you intended.

72 Let him have it

This deal arose in the qualifying rounds of a national teams championship:

West dealer : E-W vulnerable

```
        North
        ♠ Q 8 7
        ♡ Q 10 8 5
        ◇ A K 3
        ♣ Q 4 3
West              East
♠ - - -           ♠ K 9 5
♡ J 4             ♡ K 7 2
◇ J 10 9 8 6 4    ◇ Q 7 5 2
♣ J 10 9 8 2      ♣ A K 6
        South
        ♠ A J 10 6 4 3 2
        ♡ A 9 6 3
        ◇ - - -
        ♣ 7 5
```

West	North	East	South
Pass	1♣	1NT	4♠
Pass	Pass	Pass	

Lead: ♣J

West leads the ♣J, ducked all round. East takes the next club with the king and continues with the ♣A.

East is marked with almost all the high cards, including the ♠K. If you ruff the third club how do you reach dummy to take the spade finesse?

As the cards lie, leading a low heart to the ten works. That forces out the ♡K and you can cross to the ♡Q later and lead the ♠Q to trap East's ♠K.

There is a better line of play. Let East hold the third club, on which South discards a heart. Holding the major suit kings, East cannot prevent declarer reaching dummy. If necessary, declarer can discard the other heart losers on the diamond winners in dummy.

Ruffing the third club and playing a low heart to the ten could fail if East has ♡K-J bare. East could win with the jack and exit with the ♡K, depriving declarer of an entry to dummy (East can ruff the third heart). The same defence would beat 4♠ if East had ♡K-J-x and spades were 2-1.

What's the difference between teams and pairs strategy?
Answer: At teams you have to justify your actions to three players instead of just one.

Safety play: A clever way to guard against a bad break in trumps, which costs you the contract when trumps break normally.

73 Give it to him

Playing Swiss Pairs you have to bid your games and slams. The weaker the field the more you pick up simply by bidding and making laydown contracts. That is the flaw in this kind of event. If you are on the wrong side of most of the games, you are at the mercy of the opponents and your results can be poor even if you have played well. This deal comes from a national Swiss Pairs:

West dealer : N-S vulnerable

```
              North
              ♠ K 7
              ♡ A Q 2
              ◇ Q 7 5 2
              ♣ K Q 9 3
West                        East
♠ J 6                       ♠ 8 5 3
♡ K J 9 8 3                 ♡ 7 6
◇ J 10 6                    ◇ K 9 4 3
♣ 7 6 5                     ♣ J 10 8 2
              South
              ♠ A Q 10 9 4 2
              ♡ 10 5 4
              ◇ A 8
              ♣ A 4
```

After North opened a 15-17 1NT, South ended in 6♠ on the ◇J lead, low from dummy and taken with the ace. After three rounds of trumps, North discarding a heart, declarer played ◇8: 6 – 5 – 9. The slam can now be made via the heart finesse or by leading the ◇Q from dummy to pin West's ◇10.

There is a superior line, on the perfectly reasonable assumption that East has the ◇K. Duck the lead in dummy and win with the ◇A. Draw trumps and continue with ♣A, ♣K, ♣Q, discarding the losing diamond. Now play off the fourth club.

When clubs are 4-3 and East has the fourth club, discard a heart and let East hold the trick. As the cards lie, East is end-played and has to give you the twelfth trick in one red suit or the other. If East exits with a low diamond, you have to decide whether to play East for the ◇K or West for the ♡K.

If East shows out on the fourth club, you ruff and lead a low heart to the queen. This will succeed if West has the ♡K or if East holds ♡K-J(-x-x) as well as the ◇K.

74 Double your pleasure, double your fun, Give yourself two chances instead of just one.

Most pairs would find their way to 6NT on this deal:

South dealer : E-W vulnerable

```
          North
          ♠ K 10 6
          ♡ A Q 8
          ◇ A J 9 3
          ♣ A Q J
West               East
♠ J 7 5 2          ♠ 8 4 3
♡ J 10 5           ♡ K 4 3
◇ 10 5 2           ◇ 8 6 4
♣ 9 6 2            ♣ 10 7 5 4
          South
          ♠ A Q 9
          ♡ 9 7 6 2
          ◇ K Q 7
          ♣ K 8 3
```

West	North	East	South
			1NT
Pass	6NT	All pass	

Lead: ♣6

The small slam is all right, but nothing special. Just as well that South has a maximum 1NT. If South did not have the ◇Q, the slam would be a poor bet, despite the 33 HCP. That is because a 4-3-3-3 pattern has such poor playing strength. With a 4-3-3-3 facing a 4-3-3-3 you need lots of points for success.

Take no credit if your plan was to take the heart finesse. That will work 50% of the time, but you can improve your chances by taking two finesses.

Start by playing a low heart towards dummy. If West plays low, play the ♡8. On the actual deal, this will force out the king and you are home. If the ♡8 lost, you would finesse the ♡Q next time. Swap the hearts in the East-West hands and you will see how the two finesses work for you.

If East has K-10-x or K-J-x in hearts you are doomed. You can succeed double dummy if East has ♡K-10-x-x or ♡K-J-x-x or more, as long as East does not have more than four cards in diamonds or more than three in any other suit, but how can you tell that?

Pre-empt: A bid designed to stop the opponents making their usual mistakes.

Pre-emptive jump-raise: A very weak bid designed to test partner's declarer play and patience.

75   South dealer : North-South vulnerable

North
- ♠ J 8 7 4
- ♡ A J 7 6 3
- ♢ - - -
- ♣ J 7 5 4

South
- ♠ Q 9 5 3
- ♡ 2
- ♢ K J 9 8 7 5 4 2
- ♣ - - -

West	North	East	South
			Pass
1♡ (1)	Pass	2♣	3♢
Dble	Pass	Pass	Pass

(1) Playing 4-card Acol

West leads the ♣A. How would you play the trumps? How will you tackle the spades?

76   Teams : North dealer : Nil vulnerable

North
- ♠ Q 10 8 7 3
- ♡ A 9 5
- ♢ J
- ♣ K 8 5 2

South
- ♠ J 9 4
- ♡ K 3 2
- ♢ A 9 8 6 5
- ♣ A Q

South is in 4♠ after a 1NT opening and a transfer sequence. The lead is the ♡7. Plan the play.

77   Teams : North dealer : East-West vulnerable

North
- ♠ J 3
- ♡ Q 8 7 5
- ◇ K Q J
- ♣ A J 6 4

South
- ♠ A 10 8 7 6 5 2
- ♡ A J 2
- ◇ A 8 3
- ♣ - - -

West	North	East	South
	1♣	Pass	1♠
Pass	1NT	2♣ (1)	4♠
Pass	Pass	Pass	

(1) Genuine club suit

West leads the ♣7. Plan the play.

78   East dealer : North-South vulnerable

North
- ♠ Q 7 6 2
- ♡ K 9 6 5
- ◇ A 4
- ♣ Q 9 2

South
- ♠ A 10 5 4
- ♡ Q 8 7 4 2
- ◇ K 8
- ♣ A J

West	North	East	South
		Pass	1♡
Pass	3◇ (1)	Pass	4♡
Pass	Pass	Pass	

(1) 10-12 points, 4+ hearts

West leads the ♠8: two – jack – ace. Plan the play.

79   West dealer : Nil vulnerable

North
♠ A J 7 6 4 2
♡ A J 9 3
♢ 2
♣ Q 7

South
♠ K
♡ 10 6 5
♢ A 10 9 6
♣ K J 10 9 2

West	North	East	South
Pass	1♠	2♢	2NT
Pass	3♡	Pass	3NT
Pass	Pass	Pass	

West leads the ♢4 Plan the play.

80   East dealer : Nil vulnerable

North
♠ Q J 10 7
♡ A K 8 7
♢ 6
♣ J 9 8 3

South
♠ - - -
♡ Q
♢ A K Q 9 3 2
♣ A 10 7 6 4 2

South is in 6♣, no opposition bidding. West leads the ♠4:
queen – ace – ruffed. Plan the play.

75 The pin is mightier than the axe

On this deal from a Butler Trials championship, declarer picked all the cards right to make his doubled contract:

South dealer : N-S vulnerable

```
            North
            ♠ J 8 7 4
            ♡ A J 7 6 3
            ◇ - - -
            ♣ J 7 5 4
West                    East
♠ A 10 6 2              ♠ K
♡ Q 10 9 4             ♡ K 8 5
◇ 10 3                 ◇ A Q 6
♣ A K Q               ♣ 10 9 8 6 3 2
            South
            ♠ Q 9 5 3
            ♡ 2
            ◇ K J 9 8 7 5 4 2
            ♣ - - -
```

West	North	East	South
			Pass
1♡ (1)	Pass	2♣	3◇
Dble	Pass	Pass	Pass

(1) Playing 4-card Acol

Lead: ♣A

Influenced by the 4-card spade holding and doubt as to the appropriate level, South chose not to pre-empt. West's double was for takeout and East left it in. 3NT or 5♣ by East would have been more successful.

Declarer ruffed the club lead and, hoping to pin a singleton queen, played the ◇K, taken by East. The next club was ruffed and South now played the ◇J. This time the pin did puncture the defence, with West's ◇10 falling under the jack. This held South's trump losers to two.

The diamond layout made it clear that West's double was for takeout. Hence declarer played West to hold four spades and started with the ♠Q. He later finessed West for the ♠10 and so lost only two spade tricks.

Making 3◇ doubled scored 670. That was worth 15 Imps as the datum was E-W 430.

Want to improve your declarer play? Overbidding regularly makes excellent play essential.

Unlucky break: An opponent held all eight missing trumps.

Phantom sacrifice: An idiocy when committed by partner, an unforeseeable lie of the cards when committed by you.

Point count: A method whereby one can rationalise one's bidding errors scientifically.

76 Flaw Plan

North dealer : Nil vulnerable

North
- ♠ Q 10 8 7 3
- ♡ A 9 5
- ◊ J
- ♣ K 8 5 2

West
- ♠ A 6 5 2
- ♡ 8 7 6
- ◊ Q 4 3 2
- ♣ J 4

East
- ♠ K
- ♡ Q J 10 4
- ◊ K 10 7
- ♣ 10 9 7 6 3

South
- ♠ J 9 4
- ♡ K 3 2
- ◊ A 9 8 6 5
- ♣ A Q

A national teams championship: 4♠ by South after 1NT and a transfer sequence. Lead: ♡7

Apart from two spades, South has to deal with a heart loser and the fourth round of clubs. Some fine declarers slipped, and gave West a chance to shine, via this sequence: Win ♡K; cash ♣A, ♣Q; heart to ♡A; ♣K, ditching the losing heart. West ruffed the ♣K and had to decide what to play next.

A heart or a diamond will allow 4♠ home, but two Wests continued with a low spade to East's king. When East played a fourth club, declarer ruffed high, but West over-ruffed with the ♠A and played another spade. This took out declarer's last trump and, with a heart to lose, South was one off.

Declarer can afford to lose two spades and a heart. Dealing with dummy's losing club has a higher priority. Win with the ♡K, cash ♣A, ♣Q, then ◊A, diamond ruff with the ♠3. This is the position:

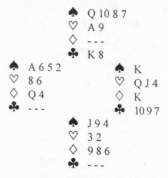

North
- ♠ Q 10 8 7
- ♡ A 9
- ◊ - - -
- ♣ K 8

West
- ♠ A 6 5 2
- ♡ 8 6
- ◊ Q 4
- ♣ - - -

East
- ♠ K
- ♡ Q J 4
- ◊ K
- ♣ 10 9 7

South
- ♠ J 9 4
- ♡ 3 2
- ◊ 9 8 6
- ♣ - - -

The ♣8 is led and ruffed with the ♠9 or ♠J. If this wins, play a heart to the ace and ruff the ♣K high. If West over-ruffs the third club and the defence can play two rounds of trumps, you are in good shape. If West over-ruffs and plays a low spade to East's king and a fourth club is played, ruff with your remaining high trump.

77 The Road to Perdition

This deal from a teams event rewarded careful play:

North dealer : E-W vulnerable

```
            North
            ♠ J 3
            ♡ Q 8 7 5
            ◇ K Q J
            ♣ A J 6 4
West                    East
♠ - - -                 ♠ K Q 9 4
♡ K 9 4 3               ♡ 10 6
◇ 10 9 7 6 5 2          ◇ 4
♣ Q 8 7                 ♣ K 10 9 5 3 2
            South
            ♠ A 10 8 7 6 5 2
            ♡ A J 2
            ◇ A 8 3
            ♣ - - -
```

West	North	East	South
	1♣	Pass	1♠
Pass	1NT	2♣ (1)	4♠
Pass	Pass	Pass	

(1) Genuine clubs

Lead: ♣7

It is easy enough to become lackadaisical and take your eye off the ball. One road to perdition is to take the ♣A, pitching a heart, and continue with the ♠3 to the ace. With the 4-0 trump break and the ♡K offside, you are one down.

As the cards lie, you could lead the ♠3 and, when East follows with the ♠4, insert the ♠8, but that is not the right line. Starting with the ♠3 fails if West began with all four spades.

At teams your concern is to make the contract. If trumps are 2-2 or 3-1, you lose at most one or two trumps and possibly a heart. The only danger is a 4-0 trump split. To guard against such a break with either opponent, ruff the club in hand and play a low spade. If West has all four trumps, you thus hold the trump losers to two.

On the actual deal West shows out and the ♠J is taken by East. When you regain the lead in dummy, you can play the ♠3 and finesse the ♠10. Again you lose just two spades and a heart.

Ruff: Cry of dismay when the trumps break badly or one of your winners is unexpectedly trumped, such as 'Ruff trick' or 'That's ruff'.

My partner and I split up because of religious differences. He thought he was the Almighty and I didn't.

78 One door shuts, another door closes

This deal comes from the 2002 New Zealand Open Teams. The popular spot was 4♡ by South and when West led the ♠8, most declarers missed a cost-free extra chance.

East dealer : N-S vulnerable

```
            North
            ♠ Q 7 6 2
            ♡ K 9 6 5
            ◇ A 4
            ♣ Q 9 2
West                    East
♠ 8 3                   ♠ K J 9
♡ A 10                  ♡ J 3
◇ 10 9 7 3              ◇ Q J 6 5 2
♣ K 8 7 4 3            ♣ 10 6 5
            South
            ♠ A 10 5 4
            ♡ Q 8 7 4 2
            ◇ K 8
            ♣ A J
```

West	North	East	South
		Pass	1♡
Pass	3◇ (1)	Pass	4♡
Pass	Pass	Pass	

(1) 10-12 points, 4+ hearts

Lead: ♠8

On the low spade from dummy, East plays the ♠J and declarer wins with the ace. To duck would work as the cards lie but that could be very foolish if the lead were a singleton. Those who played a trump at trick 2 paid the price. West took the ace, played a second spade to East's king and ruffed the spade return. They later scored a club trick for one down.

If you recall Problem #71, you will have no trouble here. Strip the diamonds before starting on the trumps and the contract is cold. Win the ♠A, cash the ◇K and ◇A and only then lead a trump. West can take the ♡A, play a spade and receive the ruff but then is endplayed. A club or a diamond exit removes your club loser.

Those who cannot remember the past are condemned to repeat it. (George Santayana)

State of the match: a phrase used in the post-mortem to excuse your normal losing decisions.

Squeeze: A play where the last card in your hand has mysteriously become a winner just as you were about to concede one off.

Some bridge players are slower than a herd of turtles stampeding through treacle.

79 Strange stranger

There were several strange choices on this deal, which arose in the final of a national teams championship:

West dealer : Nil vulnerable

```
           North
           ♠ A J 7 6 4 2
           ♡ A J 9 3
           ◇ 2
           ♣ Q 7
West              East
♠ Q 8 5 3         ♠ 10 9
♡ Q 4 2           ♡ K 8 7
◇ J 8 4           ◇ K Q 7 5 3
♣ 6 5 3           ♣ A 8 4
           South
           ♠ K
           ♡ 10 6 5
           ◇ A 10 9 6
           ♣ K J 10 9 2
```

West	North	East	South
Pass	1♠	2◇?	2NT
Pass	3♡	Pass	3NT
Pass	Pass	Pass	
Lead: ◇4			

Opposite a passed partner East's 2◇ overcall on such a poor suit and a balanced hand was sporting, indeed. Had South passed and North re-opened with a double, South would pass for penalties and collect 500 comfortably.

Having reached 3NT, it seems routine to make nine tricks via four clubs, two spades, one heart, one diamond and one extra trick somewhere along the line, probably in diamonds or hearts. It seems automatic to capture the ◇Q with the ace and immediately play a club to the queen.

Declarer took her eye off the ball when she won the ◇A and led the ♡10 at trick 2. What would this achieve? If West ducks this and East wins, East can set up an extra diamond trick (via a low diamond to the jack and a diamond back) with the ♣A still as entry.

In fact, West covered the ♡10 with the ♡Q and dummy's ace won. Next came the ♣Q, taken by the ace. A low diamond went to the jack and a diamond was returned. Now declarer had no entry to reach the ♠A and East had the ♡K as entry for the extra diamond winner. One down, −50.

If your partner makes a fool of himself, accept it as a definite improvement.

80 The stuff screams are made of

The play on this deal from the final of a teams championship left much to be desired:

East dealer : Nil vulnerable

```
          North
          ♠ Q J 10 7
          ♡ A K 8 7
          ♦ 6
          ♣ J 9 8 3
West                     East
♠ K 9 8 4 2              ♠ A 6 5 3
♡ J 5 4 3 2              ♡ 10 9 6
♦ 10 8 4                 ♦ J 7 5
♣ - - -                  ♣ K Q 5
          South
          ♠ - - -
          ♡ Q
          ♦ A K Q 9 3 2
          ♣ A 10 7 6 4 2
```

One N-S reached 5♣ via an unconvincing auction. The other N-S did better to land in 6♣, only to be undone in the play.

West led a low spade to the ace, ruffed by South, who now played the ♣A. One down, –50.

The chance of East having all three clubs is only 11% but it costs nothing to guard against that. Ruff the lead, overtake the ♡Q in dummy and lead the ♣J. If East plays the ♣5, you simply play low from hand.

If clubs are 2-1, you lose this trick, but capture the remaining trump with the ♣A later. When the ♣J holds, cash the ♣A and then set about the diamonds.

To guard against the three trumps with East, any club from dummy would work. You should choose the ♣J in order to tempt an indiscreet cover-an-honour-with-an-honour from ♣Q-5 or ♣K-5. If you meet such a defender, you would make all thirteen tricks.

Dummy: The one who would have made the contract.

Cue-bid: A slam move that partner did not understand.

Dealer: The player who has the first opportunity to blunder.

Bridge: A game for four players who will be former friends.

Dummy hand: A collection of cards which, when revealed, causes the other players to ask for a review of the bidding.

Dummy: To be stuck in partner's mouth after each hand before his standard comment is made.

Faint heart ne'er won fair contract.